Ancient Egyptian

Mummies

A Very Peculiar History™

With added Mushy Bits

'As for all men who shall
enter this my tomb...there will be
judgement...an end shall be made
for him...I shall seize his neck like
a bird...I shall cast the fear of myself
into him.'

Inscription found in tomb of
Khentika Ikhekhi (6th dynasty)

Book House

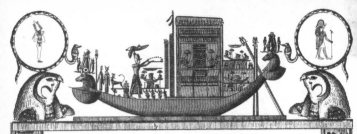

To Meliss, a great Mummy (and beautifully preserved)
Jim

Editor: Jamie Pitman

Published in Great Britain in MMXIV by
Book House, an imprint of
The Salariya Book Company Ltd
25 Marlborough Place, Brighton BN1 1UB
www.salariya.com
www.book-house.co.uk

HB ISBN: 978-1-909645-08-0

1 3 5 7 9 8 6 4 2
A CIP catalogue record for this book is available
from the British Library.
Printed and bound in China.
Printed on paper from sustainable sources.

Additional artwork: Mark Bergin, Carolyn Franklin, John James,
David Salariya, Nick Spender, Lyn Stone, Shirley Willis

First published in MMIX as Ancient Egypt, A Very Peculiar History - The Art of Embalming
Mummy Myth and Magic © The Salariya Book Company Ltd.

Ancient Egyptian
Mummies
A Very Peculiar History™

With added Mushy Bits

Jim Pipe

Created and designed by
David Salariya

Illustrated by
David Antram

BOOK HOUSE
a SALARIYA imprint

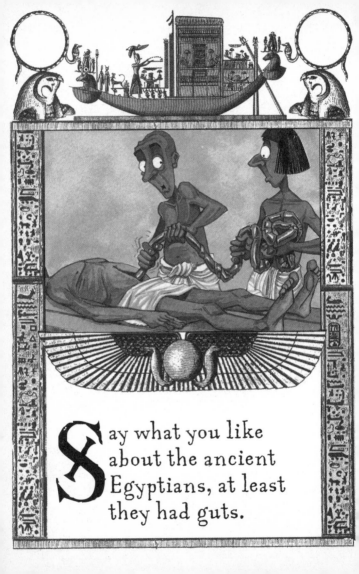

Say what you like about the ancient Egyptians, at least they had guts.

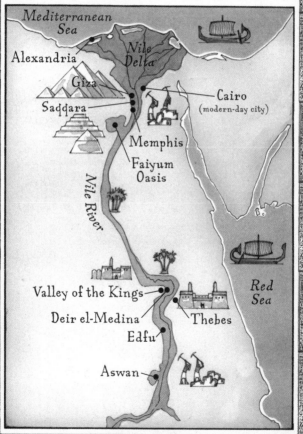

MAP DETAILING KEY AREAS AND LOCATIONS OF

ANCIENT EGYPT

Mediterranean Sea

Nile Delta

Alexandria

Giza

Saqqara

Cairo (modern-day city)

Memphis

Faiyum Oasis

Nile River

Valley of the Kings

Deir el-Medina

Thebes

Edfu

Red Sea

Aswan

Contents

Chap.		page
~	PREAMBLE: WHAT IS A MUMMY?	9
I.	WHO NEEDS A MUMMY?	17
	In which Narmer eats a crown, Anubis weighs a heart, and Ba, Ka and Akh stick around.	
II.	MAKING A MUMMY	45
	In which peasants and pharaohs get all wrapped up, and Flinders is Petrie-fied by a rattling brain.	
III.	TOMBS – A FINAL RESTING PLACE	95
	In which the dead play board games and drink beer for eternity, while the living build the first stairway to heaven.	
IV.	WAKING THE DEAD	121
	In which robbers get rich, thieves get thwarted and Tutankhamun gets a breath of fresh air.	
V.	UNWRAPPING THE SECRETS	165
	In which a tourist gets trapped, scientists get serious and Ramesses II gets his own passport.	

Ancient Egypt

A Very Peculiar History

Chap.   page
~   APPENDIX I: TIMELINE   182
         A brief chronological examination of the history
         of the ancient Egyptian civilisation and their
         mummification practices.

~   APPENDIX II: GLOSSARY   186
         A collection of definitions of terms emboldened
         within the main text.

~   INDEX   188

'You are young again.
You live again.
You are young again.
You live again.
FOREVER.'

(Ancient Egyptian prayer for the dead)

Some Famous Mummies

- King Tutankhamun (nicknamed 'King Tut') is the only Egyptian pharaoh (king) whose tomb was discovered intact. The solid gold mask and other fabulous treasures found alongside his body have amazed people the world over since their discovery in 1922.

- One of the best-known mummies in the British Museum in London is known as 'Ginger', thanks to his shock of red hair. Buried around 3600 BC, he was turned into something resembling a giant prune by the hot, dry sand that encased his body. A female mummy, known as 'Gingerella', was buried alongside him.

- According to legend, in 323 BC Alexander the Great (the king of Macedonia who conquered Persia) was buried in a golden coffin filled with white honey. This pickled his body for over 1,000 years until it was stolen.

- English philosopher Jeremy Bentham (1748-1832) asked a surgeon friend to preserve his body after he died. Seated as if he was deep in thought, his well-dressed skeleton is still on display at University College London.

WHAT IS A MUMMY?

When you hear the word 'mummy', what do you think of? King Tutankhamun buried deep in his tomb, or a stiff-legged zombie on the warpath? Until about three hundred years ago, the word was only used to describe mummies from ancient Egypt. It probably comes from the Persian word *mumiya*, which means **bitumen** or pitch. Today, we use this black, sticky substance to cover roads. So what does it have to do with ancient corpses?

It all goes back to AD 639, when the Arabs conquered Egypt. Though they banned the Egyptians from making any more mummies, they couldn't resist taking a peek inside their mysterious tombs. The bandaged bodies they discovered were covered in a black sticky goo which reminded them of bitumen, so the Arabs took the Persian word for bitumen and called these bodies *mumiya*. They were wrong, it wasn't bitumen, but as the years went by, *mumiya* turned into the English word 'mummy'.[1]

Today, however, the word 'mummy' is used to describe any person or animal whose flesh and skin has been preserved after death[2] – including the baby mammoth discovered in the icy wilderness of north-west Siberia (in northern Russia) in 2007.

1. *Not everyone agrees: some historians believe the word 'mummy' may also have come from the Egyptian* **Coptic** *word 'mum' which means wax, an important material used in mummification.*
2. *Skeletons and fossils aren't considered mummies, as no soft tissues such as flesh or skin are preserved.*

All sorts of mummies have been uncovered over the years. What makes them different from each other is how they are preserved. Some were created deliberately: the Cloud People of Peru and the Guanche people of the Canary Islands preserved their relatives after death. Other mummies were created by accident. Some bodies were pickled after being buried in sand, tar or mud. Others were freeze-dried in caves or preserved by acidic bog waters.

Normally when an animal dies, bacteria (tiny organisms in the body) eat away at the flesh until only the bones are left behind. Bacteria need water to grow, however, so if a body dries out soon after death, it stops rotting and turns into a mummy. Whether dried by chemicals, extreme cold, or the heat of the desert, a mummy can remain preserved for thousands of years. Remarkably, some mummies have leathery skin and joints that can still be moved.

In figures

- The weight of King Tutankhamun's funeral death mask, mummified body, three coffins and stone **sarcophagus** (outer container) was **1.36 tonnes** of wood, gold, precious stones (and Tut)!

- Most mummies don't have a weight problem. Once stripped of bandages, they weigh around **2-3 kilos**.

- When an 11th-**Dynasty** man named Ipy was put in his tomb, he was buried next to the **76 jars** of waste fluids and powders that had been used to mummify his body.

- One mummy was covered in **845 square metres** of linen, enough to cover three tennis courts.

- Though many mummies have already turned to dust or been destroyed, more than **500 million** may still be preserved in undiscovered tombs and burial places (and that's just in Egypt).

Though mummies have been found all over the world, Egyptian mummies have always grabbed the headlines. They were famous even in ancient times, when the Greek travellers Herodotus and Diodorus Siculus brought amazing tales of the dead back from the banks of the Nile. When the Romans conquered Egypt, they wanted to learn the secrets of the Egyptian mummymakers. Unfortunately, they couldn't read the ancient Egyptian tomb writing, hieroglyphics.[3] The famous Queen Cleopatra was also fascinated by the ancient Egyptians. Although from a Greek family, she learnt the Egyptian language and copied the ancient style of dress, perhaps to remind other Egyptians that she was one of them.

In more modern times, it was the Victorians who really sparked an interest in ancient Egypt. In the 19th century, wealthy English tourists travelling to Egypt brought back mummies as holiday souvenirs. Then they

3. *Things went from bad to worse when in 48 BC Julius Caesar accidentally set fire to the famous library at Alexandria, on the Egyptian coast, which contained thousands of ancient scrolls.*

invited all their friends round for a party to watch while the mummy was unwrapped. The Victorians also loved reading scary stories about mummies coming back from the dead – stories that movie audiences still enjoy today.

By the 20th century, spooky stories gave way to serious study. People began to appreciate that these amazing relics were once living people. They wanted to learn more about how the ancient Egyptians lived, and why they took so much trouble to prepare for the afterlife. Experts known as **Egyptologists** carefully studied the ancient texts written on tomb walls and coffins, while X-rays allowed them to investigate mummies without damaging them.

In the 1932 horror film *The Mummy*, the bandaged monster was based on the mummy of pharaoh Seti I.

It seems that the Egyptians enjoyed life so much they wanted it to go on forever – even after they died. However, they believed their soul couldn't enter heaven unless their body lasted too. That's why Egyptian mummymakers, or embalmers,[4] turned dead Egyptians into mummies to preserve them. Amazing tombs were built for the dead to live in – often more beautiful than the buildings meant to house living people – and kings were buried with fabulous treasures to enjoy after death.

With each new discovery comes a better understanding of this remarkable, and very peculiar, world. Yet mysterious elements remain, from the magic spells and amulets used to protect a mummy to the deadly traps and pits designed to outwit wily tomb robbers. Enter at your peril!

4. The word 'embalmer' comes from 'balsam', the sweet-smelling oils that were rubbed on dead bodies to help preserve them.

WARNING!

Time to confess. There's no avoiding the fact that turning a stinking corpse into a mummy is a mucky business (there's a lot more to it than stuffing an animal, for instance). However, if reading about blood and guts makes you queasy, the **LOOK AWAY** signs will help you avoid the really mushy bits.

CHAPTER ONE

WHO NEEDS A MUMMY?

On the Banks of the Nile

Before we get into the gruesome details of how the Egyptians pickled themselves for eternity, let's find out a bit more about these remarkable people, and why they put so much energy into burying their dead.

If you were an ancient Egyptian living at the time of King Tutankhamun (around 1330 BC), your ancestors had already been living in Egypt for some 40,000 years. The first Egyptians were hunters roaming around what is now the Sahara desert. Tens of thousands of years ago, this wilderness was covered in grass

and echoed with the sounds of wild lions, gazelles, buffaloes and ostriches going about their business.

Around 10,000 BC, the climate changed and the rains began to dry up.[1] As the grasslands turned into the giant desert we know today, the Egyptians headed for the wetlands of the Nile Valley. During the Stone Age, the families of hunters and fishermen lived along the river banks. At first, the surrounding valley was swampy and overgrown with trees, reeds and rushes, but they gradually cleared the swamps and built villages. By 5000 BC, the Egyptians had learned how to farm and grow crops in the rich soil. They built houses with mud bricks and learned how to make glass and work metals such as copper and gold. The Nile was their highway and they built fine ships and boats by lashing reeds together.[2]

1. While the Egyptian plains were drying up, rain and snow falling on the forests and mountains to the south turned the Nile into a great torrent that carved its way through the sandy hills towards the Mediterranean.
2. Even though Asian invaders known as the Hyksos introduced the Egyptians to chariots around 1650–1550 BC, wheels never really caught on and the Egyptians continued to move goods on land the slow way: on donkeys or wooden sledges pulled by oxen.

Milk, butter, cheese, figs, grapes and meat – all in a day's work.

These early Egyptians were very organised. They worked together to control the Nile, building **dykes** and canals to help water their land and grow more crops. Villages grew into towns and cities. These were important trading centres and sacred sites as well as being a safe haven from warlike neighbours and bandits. A steady supply of food meant the Egyptians had more time to enjoy life: by 4000 BC they were wearing make-up... (Egyptian men, women and children decorated their faces).

Early on, each city had its own chieftain or king. Through a combination of war, conquest and agreement these small states merged into two kingdoms, Upper and Lower Egypt, known as 'the two lands'. Around 3100 BC, Egypt was unified under one ruler, King Narmer, the first to wear both the white crown of Upper Egypt and the red crown of Lower Egypt.[3]

3. An ancient text, the 'cannibal hymn', shows the pharaoh eating the crown of Lower Egypt to symbolise his power over the the land.

The Mighty Pharaohs

Narmer's rule marked the beginning of written history in Egypt. The kings that came after him, the pharaohs, are so numerous that they are grouped into 30 families, or dynasties. A dynasty can have as many as 14 kings or just one. The 30th and final dynasty ended with the death of Cleopatra in 30 BC, when Egypt became part of the Roman Empire.

To make Egypt's long, long history[4] easier to understand, the dynasties are also grouped into three peaceful periods known as the Old Kingdom (2686–2160 BC), Middle Kingdom (2040–1633 BC), and New Kingdom (1558–1085 BC), broken up by shorter spells of civil war and invasion, known as the Intermediate Periods. In fact, much of ancient Egypt's history was remarkably peaceful.

---

4. To get a sense of just how long the ancient Egyptians were around, remember that when the ancient Greek historian Herodotus visited Egypt around 450 BC, the pyramids were already over 2,500 years old.

Top Pharaohs

- **Khufu/Cheops** (4th Dynasty), who built the great pyramid at Giza, the only one of the ancient wonders of the world still standing.

- **Khafre/Khephren** (4th Dynasty), who built the sphinx and the second pyramid at Giza.

- **Tuthmosis III** (18th Dynasty), a small man (1.5 m tall) but a brilliant general who created a vast Egyptian Empire and oversaw a great temple-building programme.

- **Akhenaten** (18th Dynasty), the '**heretic**' king, who tried to change Egypt's religion after saying there was only one god, Aten.

- **Hatshepsut** (18th Dynasty), a very successful queen who crowned herself as pharaoh and had a long and prosperous reign.

- **Ramesses II 'the Great'** (19th Dynasty), a warrior who ruled for 66 years and had over 100 sons. His mummy was found reburied in the tomb of Amenhotep II.

- **Queen Cleopatra VII** (30th Dynasty), who committed suicide using poison, possibly snake venom, after her fleet was destroyed by the Romans and her lover Mark Antony had killed himself.

A Magical Kingdom

By the New Kingdom it's already some 1,800 years since the time of King Narmer, but life has hardly changed at all. Egyptians farm and dress much as their ancestors did all those generations before. They also think very much like them. This is partly due to where they live. Egypt is cut off from the world: by deserts to the east and west, dangerous waterfalls and rapids to the south, and the swampy Nile **delta** to the north.

The Egyptians live in a rich and prosperous land blessed with hot sun and a good water supply, ideal for growing crops. Once a year, the mighty Nile floods when the spring snows melt in the mountains to the south. For four months its waters cover a strip of land a few kilometres wide. When the floodwaters retreat, they leave behind a layer of rich black mud that fertilises the crops in the following year. Because of this, Egyptians call their land *Kemet*, or 'the Black Land'. They look down on their neighbours in Libya and Nubia, who scratch a living from the desert.

The Egyptians believe their life is perfect – there is no need for change. To them, the annual flood is a magical event, as it hardly ever rains in Egypt[5] and the country is completely surrounded by *Deshret* ('the Red Land' or desert). The difference between the two is shocking – you can stand with one foot on the rich black soil and the other foot in the lifeless red sand where nothing grows. So the miracle of the yearly flood can only be the work of the gods. Egyptians even worship the flood itself in form of Hapy, a bearded god with water-plants sprouting from his head and the breasts of a woman.

The ancient Egyptian flood god was always Hapy to help.

5. *Today, the skies above Egypt remain sunny and cloudless all year round and there is almost no rainfall in Upper Egypt.*

If that's not enough to make them believe in magic, each day the Egyptians witness another miracle as the sun rises in the east and sets in the west. This is the sun god Amun Re (also king of the gods) travelling across the sky in a boat. No wonder the Egyptians believe they are blessed. Keep the gods happy, and the good life will continue. Anger them, and disaster will surely follow!

The pharaoh makes daily offerings to the god Re on behalf on his people, to ensure that the sun will rise again the next day. A ruler and a living god, the pharaoh is all-powerful. It's his job to bring harmony to the universe by preserving *ma'at* (order). It's a big job for one person, so the pharaoh is helped by the teams of priests that work in the great temples such as Karnak and Edfu. They read prayers, sing hymns and offer food to images of the gods. Large temples even have their own choirs, musicians and dancers, who perform wild acrobatic acts.

Seven Wonders of Ancient Egypt

1. **Buildings** – The Step pyramid at Saqqara was the first large stone building in the world. The Great Pyramid at Giza was made from 2,300,000 stone blocks, each weighing an incredible 2.5 tonnes.

2. **Writing** – Egyptians invented writing some time before 3000 BC. Their hieroglyphics were holy symbols used for wall carvings and pictures. Hieratic script was a simpler version used for writing on scrolls.

3. **Mathematics** – Being whizzes at maths helped the Egyptians become great builders. The Great Pyramid is only around 0.05 per cent off being a perfect square.

4. **Astronomy** – Egyptians worked out that there are 365 days in a year. The star map created by Senmut, vizier (the most important official) to Queen Hatshepsut, also shows that the Egyptians were able to predict the movement of the planets across the sky.

5. **Food** – Egyptians invented the first bakeries and the first sweets, which were made from dates and spices. Their workers ate the first packed lunches, too – bread, beer and onions.

6. **Fashion** – Ancient Egyptians wore make-up (eyeshadow and lipstick), wigs made from human hair, and tattoos. Their shoes were made of leather, wood and even sheet gold. Despite the heat, posh Egyptians were among the first to wear gloves.

7. **Gadgets** – Egyptian architects used a plumb-line: a heavy weight on the end of a piece of string that, thanks to gravity, always hung in a straight line. This ensured any buildings were 'plumb' (perfectly upright). Around 1500 BC, an Egyptian court official named Amenemhet invented the first water clock.

Extracts from Senmut's Star Map

Senmut's 'star map' features figures that represent constellations. The bull is the constellation now known as the Plough.

Planning for Death

The ancient Egyptian belief in life after death may have come from their wonder at seeing the sun rise each morning. Perhaps they were convinced after discovering that bodies buried on the edge of the desert were miraculously preserved after death. We will never know for sure, but about 6,000 years ago, the Egyptians began to bury their dead in graves and tombs.

Model mummies handed round during Egyptian feasts: the first ever game of 'Pass the Parcel'?

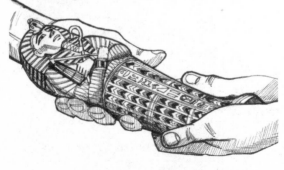

28

The Egyptians undoubtedly spent a lot of time thinking about death – during toasts at feasts they passed round models of mummies to remind themselves that death was never far away. But you'd be wrong to think that they were a miserable bunch who had nothing better to do. In their writings, they come across as lively, jolly people. Every funeral text contained a song that stressed the importance of enjoying life while waiting to enter the Otherworld, or 'the land that loves silence':

> Follow your heart while you live!
> Enjoy your holidays!
> Make your things on earth!
> No-one can take his things with him.
> Look, no-one who has gone there
>   comes back.

Maybe the Egyptians enjoyed life so much that they never wanted it to end. Sadly, it often did while they were still young. In ancient times, if you lived to 40, you were doing well. Though ancient Egyptian doctors were ahead of their time, they couldn't stop a

child dying from a bad cold. So instead of planning for old age, the Egyptians planned for the life after death. They did everything they could to ensure a smooth journey into the next world. The alternative was just too horrible to think about.

The Egyptian idea of death, heaven and hell changed over the centuries. In the Old Kingdom, the Egyptians believed that the pharaoh either travelled to the stars to live with the gods or accompanied the sun on its daily voyage across the sky. As long as he survived the journey into the afterlife – thanks to a well-equipped pyramid – he would carry the rest of the country along with him to eternity.

By the time of the Middle Kingdom, you had to behave yourself while you were alive. Not even the pharaoh could assume he would automatically reach the Otherworld, now thought to be an underground kingdom ruled over by Osiris, the 'Lord of all Eternity'.

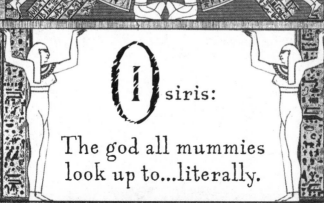

Osiris:

The god all mummies
look up to...literally.

New Kingdom Egyptians believed that living a good life was more important than wealth in booking a ticket to the Otherworld. Around 300 BC, the high priest Petosiris wrote that this was the only way to reach the afterlife successfully. Yet most Egyptians continued to build the most lavish tombs they could afford – just in case!

The Very first Mummy

In Egyptian myth, the god Osiris was tricked into a trunk by his dastardly brother Seth. Seth then threw the trunk into the Nile, drowning Osiris. He didn't stop there: after Osiris' wife, the goddess Isis, found the body, Seth stole it and hacked it to pieces. Poor Isis then collected up all the bits and, with help from her sister Nephtys, pieced them back together. Anubis, the jackal-headed god, then embalmed Osiris. Using magic, Anubis brought Osiris back to life, setting the standard for all other mummies. Every Egyptian wanted to follow Osiris' example and conquer death.

For the rich, the journey to the Otherworld was a lifetime's work. As well as building a chapel and a tomb you had to pay for coffins, masks, jars to store removed organs, and a mass of furniture and other belongings.[6] A tomb was probably a noble's biggest expense and a source of great pride. When King Amenemhet I wrote to his son Sesostris, he boasted how fine his tomb was, not his palace. The poor, however, had to make do with a basic tomb, a few grave goods, mummification on the cheap and a cut-price inscription on the walls.

Most of the finest Egyptian tombs were built while their occupants were still alive. Someone who had lived a long life would have equipped his tomb right down to the last detail and even written his own life story and **epitaph** for the tomb walls. All his heirs had to do was to provide daily offerings after his death.

---

6. *If an Egyptian died suddenly, his or her relatives were expected to bury the body properly. If they didn't, they couldn't inherit anything from the dead person.*

Most Egyptians agreed that a well-preserved body was the best way to achieve life after death. Once dead, your body was a gateway that allowed food offerings and the magic spells on the walls of a tomb to travel with you into the Otherworld. Ideally, your body was protected from rotting by being turned into a mummy. It was now known as *sah* and became a new, perfectly formed body 'filled with magic' that would last for eternity. But if part of your body had been damaged in any way (perhaps you were unlucky enough to have been chomped on by a crocodile), a sculpture or painting could show the missing details.

If the very worst happened and your body was completely destroyed, then speaking your name after death was enough to ensure your survival in the afterlife. You just needed to be famous enough for people to keep saying your name for thousands of years after you died. Many pharaohs left behind hundreds of statues and inscriptions so their name would never be forgotten. These were sometimes vandalised by their successors in an attempt to destroy them in the Otherworld!

The Journey to the Otherworld

The Egyptians believed your body was made up of different forms. As well as your physical body, your name and your shadow were a 'living' part of you.[7] Your soul had three different forms: *Ba*, *Ka* and *Akh*, all of which would be set free from your body when you died.

If your *Ba*, *Ka* and *Akh* were going to work properly after death, your body had to survive in one piece. Only then could your *Akh* reach the Fields of Reeds (*Aaru*), the ancient Egyptian heaven. Ruled by Osiris, this was like a perfect version of Egypt, a wonderful place where lush fields stretched as far as the eye could see and an army of servants tended to your every need.

7. *The ancient Egyptians believed that when you died, your shadow, or shewt, separated from the body and whizzed around on its own at great speed. Priests and relatives said prayers which protected it from harmful demons, as destroying someone's shadow would wipe them out forever.*

Guide to the Soul

The **Ba** was your personality, or character. It lived in the tomb but was free to come and go. It often visited the land of the living, where it usually took the form of a bird.

BA

The **Ka** was your life force and it looked exactly like you. It had to stay close to your body and within the tomb for the rest of eternity. The *Ka* required food, drink and clothing and so it relied on a steady supply of offerings.

KA

The **Akh** was the part of your soul that lived on in the Otherworld for eternity. At the moment of death, the *Akh* left the body and flew to the stars to spend eternity in the heavens, sailing in the boat of the sun god Re or living with King Osiris in the Fields of Reeds.

In the Old Kingdom, only the *Akh* of a pharaoh could have the enjoyment of reaching the Fields of Reeds. Everyone else had no choice but to mope around for eternity haunting their own gloomy tomb. As a result, rich nobles in the Old Kingdom built deluxe tombs kitted out with everything that money could buy. If they couldn't get to the Fields of Reeds, they might as well spend eternity in a luxurious tomb.

By the 2nd dynasty, the Egyptians found a cheaper way of making sure they had everything they needed in the afterlife – magic! By the 3rd dynasty, more and more space in tombs was taken up with spells, along with pictures and models of what was needed.

During the Middle Kingdom, rich nobles and then merchants and farmers claimed the right to enter heaven. Soon every Egyptian town had its own city of the dead, or 'necropolis', where ordinary citizens were buried with jewellery, weapons and fine pottery.

By the time of the New Kingdom, the Fields of Reeds were open to anyone – but with one small condition. After death your *Akh* headed west into the fearsome Sahara[8] and into an underground labyrinth of gates and doors. It could only enter the Fields of Reeds if it survived this long, perilous journey through the Otherworld, a parallel universe where the Sun travelled across the sky at night.

Long passages in the tombs of the Valley of the Kings (a valley which was used for burying the most important pharaohs and nobles) are decorated with scenes showing the *Akh*'s journey. They reveal a maze of obstacles – rivers, mountains and caverns – where gods and monsters lurked. The Egyptians were genuinely terrified by the thought of meeting Otherworld demons such as the 15-metre-long serpent that lived in the the Mountain of Bakhu.

8. *The Sahara desert was a real-life terror, inhabited by hostile tribes as well as lions, leopards, snakes and scorpions. Desert travellers also brought back tales of demons and monsters that became real in the minds of the Egyptians.*

To get through this labyrinth, your *Akh* had to answer a barrage of questions from gate-keepers and the magical gates themselves. Forgetful? Don't worry, most Egyptians were buried with a crib – a complete set of questions and answers which also acted as a passport and ensured a warm welcome by Osiris.

The Old Kingdom pharaohs were buried with *Pyramid Texts*, a series of spells to protect the dead king on his journey through the Otherworld. By the Middle Kingdom, a set of spells were conveniently painted on the side of the coffin (giving them their name, *Coffin Texts*). In the New Kingdom, a scroll was placed in the tomb or inside a mummy's wrappings. Egyptians knew these spells as *Coming Forth by Day*, but today they often go by the far spookier title, *The Book of the Dead*.

The scroll listed many of the spells needed to survive the afterlife, as well as hymns of praise to charm the various gods your *Akh* might meet on its journey, such as Osiris, Re and Hathor. Simply having *The Book of the Dead* alongside your mummy was enough to ensure survival in the afterlife. Other scrolls have been found in royal tombs, such as *The Book of Gates* and *The Book of Caverns*, but historians think that these were probably more for decoration. Once your *Akh* had made it safely through the labyrinth it reached the hall of judgement. Here 42 gods sat on an interview panel waiting to test you. Your *Akh* made a series of set speeches saying what an absolutely fabulous person you were and what a good life you had led while alive:

> I've made no man hungry,
> I have not carried away milk from
> the mouths of children,
> I have not driven away cattle which
> were upon their pastures,
> I have not run off with cakes or
> offerings to the gods.

If you had done a few naughty things (heaven forbid!) there were spells written on the walls of your tomb or in *The Book of the Dead* that would smooth things out with the divine panel.

A Magical Passport

The Book of the Dead was not what we think of as a book but a collection of 200 or so magic spells written on a single scroll of **papyrus** (strips of reeds beaten to form long rolls like paper). One of the best-preserved copies comes from *The Papyrus of Ani*, written in 1240 BC and originally over 23 metres long. The spells help Ani's *Akh* to overcome any obstacle in its path, as well as providing him with everything he needs for a happy life in the Fields of Reeds. They give his dead body the power to:

- Speak

- Be safe from fire and water

- Transform itself into animals such as hawks, snakes and crocodiles

- Pass the 'weighing of the heart' test

- Be given cakes and ale in heaven

- Return to the land of the living and take revenge on his enemies

- Never rot away

- Look like a god. Each part of the body became like a particular god: Ani now had the eyes of Hathor, the face of Re, the cheeks of Isis, the backbone of Set, the belly of Sekhmet, the thighs of Nut and the feet of Ptah!

After answering the holy questions came the electrifying climax to your *Akh*'s journey through the Otherworld. Anubis, the jackal-headed god, solemnly weighed your heart against the feather of truth using a giant set of scales. Only the truly good would pass this final test. Thoth then scribbled down the result in his scroll. If the heart was lighter than the feather, the person passed and their *Akh* was presented to Osiris by the god Horus.

If your heart was too heavy, it was a sign that you had not led a good life. Disaster! Your heart was fed to Ammut the Gobbler, 'Eater of the Dead', a hideous monster with the head of a crocodile, the front end of a lion and the rear end of a hippo. Once eaten by Ammut, your *Akh* was doomed to haunt the living for eternity as an evil spirit.[9] Most **papyri** show people passing the test, so for the most part Ammut went hungry!

9. *Egyptians believed that spirits of the dead – ghosts – roamed the Earth at night. Pottery figures of cobras were used to ward them off.*

Phew! So your *Akh* has passed the final test and been granted a plot of land in the Fields of Reeds. Here your soul could finally relax, safe from all harm. Or could it? It was still possible to die again if your corpse got destroyed. If this happened, your *Ka*, *Ba* and *Akh* perished in turn, and your soul was obliterated forever. Of course, if you were famous enough to have people still chanting your name hundreds of years after your death, this grisly fate could be avoided, and your *Akh*'s place in the Fields of Reeds was guaranteed – at least until your fans stopped chanting your name.

All in all, maintaining a good-looking mummy was a passport to eternal life. That's why Egyptian embalmers were trained to preserve corpses in as lifelike a manner as possible. They were so successful that today we can view an Egyptian mummy and have a pretty good idea of what he or she looked like 3,000 years ago.

Do It Right

LOOK AWAY!

- Egyptians were terrified of dying abroad in case their corpse didn't get home in time for a proper burial.

- It was very important to be buried right way, clean and pure. One royal mummy has been found buried in a dirty sheepskin. Its face looks as though it was screaming with agony, so did the victim die horribly as a punishment for a terrible crime? Being buried in a dirty skin may have been part of the punishment.

- The most serious crimes, such as rebellion or treason, were sometimes punished by destroying the criminal's body. Once your body had been completely burnt to ashes or gobbled up by crocodiles, there was no hope of a proper burial or a successful journey through the Otherworld.

CHAPTER TWO

MAKING A MUMMY

Sun~Dried Corpses

Though their beliefs about death hadn't changed through the centuries, the ancient Egyptians were terrified that if their dead body began to rot, their *Ka* would go hungry and their chances of eternal life would be in real peril.

The art of making mummies, or 'embalming', was all about stopping the body from rotting. Where did the idea come from? The first Egyptian mummies were flukes – bodies preserved by accident after being buried in the hot desert sand. The dry climate sucked the bodily fluids away, rapidly drying the

corpse while preserving the flesh and organs such as the heart and liver. The stone-splitting heat baked the skin, turning it dark and hard like a roast potato. Despite this, the withered corpse left behind was still definitely human – even the hair and fingernails survived.

In time, a violent sandstorm may have disturbed some of these early graves, proving to the Egyptians that drying out a body could preserve it. Even today, thousands of years later, Egyptologists are still digging up well-preserved bodies from the 'bone-dry' desert sands.

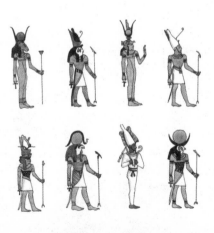

LOOK AWAY!

Dirty Rotters

When living things die, they quickly begin to rot. Rotting is caused by the tiny bacteria that our body uses to digest food and turn it into the minerals the body needs to live and grow. While we're alive, white blood cells eat and absorb the bacteria, keeping them under control. But when we die, the bacteria soon begin to outnumber the white blood cells and the rot begins.

- **Stage 1**: Within a few hours, bacteria begin to eat a body's soft internal organs.

- **Stage 2**: In a warm, damp environment a body starts to putrefy (go mushy) after about three days. Flies and other scavengers are often attracted to a rotting corpse. They lay eggs that hatch into maggots. These crawl into the body and begin to munch it.

- **Stage 3**: Over the next few months, the rotting corpse gives off gases. These attract more flies and other insects. The soft, fleshy bits start to disintegrate (break up) leaving only the skeleton and hair. In the right conditions, this can happen in just ten days.

The very first mummies created on purpose by the Egyptians date from around 3200 BC. They appear in pit graves – a simple hole in the ground which was just large enough to hold the curled-up body of the deceased and a few grave goods. The body was then covered in sand, preserving it. In time, upturned reed baskets were placed over the faces and pillows were placed behind the head to help the dead snooze in peace.

Soon richer nobles went for basketwork trays placed above and below the corpse. It wasn't long before graves began to have a lining of wood or stone and a roof (perhaps to protect the bodies from hungry desert dogs and jackals). For all their added luxury, these mini-tombs were a big mistake, as corpses were protected from the hot desert sand, which is precisely what should have preserved them. While their poor neighbours dried up nicely in the cheap pit graves, the wealthy bodies became a feast for maggots!

Cheap graves:

they're the pits!

What a Way to Go!

The Ancient Egyptians deliberately turned bodies into mummies using a salt called natron. However, there's more than one way to pickle your parents!

ACCIDENTAL

- **Chill Out!** – Ötzi the Iceman was found by a couple of mountain walkers in the Austro-Italian Alps in 1993. His 5,300-year-old body, preserved by the freezing cold, dried out over time as the moisture in it turned to ice. Despite the arrow head in his shoulder, scientists now believe Ötzi died after hitting his head on a rock, or after being bashed on the head by an attacker!

- **Ready Salted** – Freeze dried by the cold climate and salty soil, a man, three women and a baby were found buried together in the Takla Makan Desert in China. Dating from around 2000 BC, the most amazing thing about these 'Tarim' mummies is that they are not Chinese but European. They are dressed in a sort of tartan. The baby was buried with a cowhorn cup and her sheep's-udder nursing bottle. Small blue stones cover her eyes and there are tiny strands of red wool in her nostrils.

- **Bogged Down** – Several well-preserved bodies have been found in peat bogs in northwest Europe. These cold, still pools of water have high acid and low oxygen levels that help to mummify human flesh. Moss in the peat can also turn skin into leather. One body found in Ireland in 2006 was so well-preserved that police started a murder investigation – until archaeologists proved the victim was 2,000 years old!

FOR ONE NIGHT ONLY:

Ötzi is 'The Iceman' in an ancient extravaganza of preservation...

'MUMMIES ON ICE'

ON PURPOSE

- **Stuffed** – The black mummies found at Chinchorro, in northern Chile, were created around 5000 BC, making them the oldest mummies in the world. After removing the flesh from their dead relatives' bones, the Chinchorro people reinforced the skeleton with sticks before stuffing it with clay, reeds and sea grasses. The body was then covered with mud and may have been displayed in the homes of living relatives before being buried. A mask of clay was placed over the face to give the impression that it was sleeping peacefully, with slits cut for the mouth and eyes.

- **Going Green** – During the Han dynasty (206 BC to 220 AD) Chinese embalmers hoped their Emperors and nobles would live forever if they wrapped them in suits made from jade, a green semi-precious stone. They buried the mummies in deep tombs cut into the rock. Unfortunately, the jade didn't preserve the bodies, so they rotted.

- **Holy Smokes** – The Dani people of Irian Jaya, in Indonesia, preserved the bodies of their chiefs by smoking them over fires. Smoking is an ancient method of preserving meat and fish. While the heat dries the meat, chemicals in the smoke act as preservatives.

- **Starvation** – From the 17th to the 19th centuries, Buddhist priests in the Japanese Shingon sect mummified themselves while still alive. They slowly starved themselves and ate poisons to kill the bacteria that make bodies rot after death. The mummified priests were then put on display in temples to inspire the next generation of holy men.

- **Rubberised** – In the 1980s German Professor Gunther von Hagens developed a way to preserve bodies known as 'plastination'. This process involves removing the fat, water, blood and tissue from the body and replacing it with plastics such as silicone rubber, resin or polyester. The bodies are then placed into real-life poses to highlight just how amazing the human body is.

- **Deep Freeze** – Cryogenics (meaning 'creating freezing cold') uses ultra-low temperatures to store dead bodies, in the hope that they can be thawed out and cured by doctors in the future.

Gunther von Hagens' 'plastination' process turns corpses into plastic mummies!

If At first You Don't Succeed...

A cramped, smelly pit may have dried the body but it was no place for a self-respecting *Ka* to spend eternity. It was also easy to rob, unlike tombs dug deep in the sand and lined with stone blocks. So the Egyptians came up with a clever compromise – build a fabulous tomb but pickle the body. This was great in theory but hard to achieve. It took many years of clumsy trial and error to create the perfect mummy. While some experiments rotted, others turned to mush. Early attempts were often black and crumbly – later ones are yellow and rubbery!

Attempt 1 – *The dead body is simply wrapped in tight layers of bandages.*

The earliest identified Egyptian mummy dates back to the 1st Dynasty. When it was first discovered by British Egyptologist Flinders Petrie, the mummy's body had been ripped apart by grave robbers. Only a mummified wrist was left, probably belonging to the pharaoh Djer or one of his wives.

Attempt 2 – *The bandages are soaked with resin (a preservative) and padding is used to make the body look more lifelike.*

The mummies looked good, but the hard linen shell trapped moisture, making the bodies inside rot. Some mummies also had their faces painted green (to Egyptians this was the colour of rebirth rather than the colour of putrid slime).

Attempt 3 – *Bandages and plaster are used to give the body a more lifelike shape, and internal organs are removed quickly to stop the body rotting so fast.*

By the 3rd Dynasty, mummymakers were slitting open the belly, whipping out the organs,[1] then stuffing the hole with resin-soaked linen. The slit was then sealed with more resin – the same way sailors use tar to patch holes in a leaky boat. The *Pyramid Texts* reveal that the main aim of 5th-Dynasty embalmers was to keep the bones intact and to make sure the head didn't fall off!

1. *The organs were kept because they would be needed in the next life. In time, special containers were used to store them.*

Shake, Rattle and Roll

LOOK AWAY!

When the archeologist Flinders Petrie found the mummy of 4th-Dynasty High Priest Ranefer in 1890, the head had been ripped off by robbers desperate to steal its copper necklace. The head was painted, with black hair, green eyes and eyebrows and red mouth. Wanting to take a closer look, Petrie picked up the head and got a nasty shock when he heard the sound of its dried-up brain rattling around inside. Another mummy nearby had the flesh stripped from its bones before the bandages were put on. This attempt to preserve the body never caught on, probably because the resulting mummy looked so hideous!

Finally, Flinders had found something to keep the baby quiet...although mummy wouldn't be too happy.

RATTLE!

Few mummies from the Old Kingdom survive as most bodies eventually rotted below the layers of bandages. Several complete mummies have lasted from the Middle Kingdom, however, thanks to better methods of preservation. The materials used to mummify the body were now buried near the body as the Egyptians believed they might contain tiny pieces of the dead person that they would need in the Otherworld.

By the 18th dynasty, Egyptian embalmers had cracked the secret of preserving a body forever. They did their best to make mummies look as lifelike as possible, making up to 17 cuts in the body to make sure it was padded realistically. Many very well-preserved mummies survive from the New Kingdom, such as that of the pharaoh Seti I. Though more and more Egyptians were being mummified using simpler methods after 1000 BC, embalming techniques were as good as ever.

Mummification survived the arrival of both Greek (332 BC) and Roman invaders (after 30 BC). Unlike the Egyptians, the Romans had a taste for statues and paintings that looked like the real thing. They believed it was important that the mummy and coffin showed exactly how the dead person looked. Portraits were painted on top of the shroud or on thin wood panels. Some Roman-era coffin lids were also decorated with 3-D plaster portraits.

However, under the wrappings the preservation methods became less and less effective. Many of the ancient embalming skills had been lost and mummies were simply covered in a large dollop of resin. After 3,000 years, the tradition of making mummies was slowly dying out, helped in part by the spread of Christianity in the 4th century AD. By the time the Arabs invaded, 300 years later, mummies were a thing of the past.

The Romans just couldn't keep their hands off other people's religions.

Washing and Removing the Organs

Sadly, no 'how to' book remains explaining exactly how ancient Egyptian mummymakers preserved dead bodies. Maybe there never was one, as trade secrets were passed down from father to son. The best description we have is by the Greek historian Herodotus, who travelled to Egypt in the 5th century BC. He claims that three different methods were used, depending on how wealthy the dead person was.

Herodotus goes on to describe a witches' brew of oils, resins, perfumes, and even a sort of gum. Modern tests reveal few traces of these chemicals, including the bitumen, or *mumiya*, that gives mummies their name. Also, we can't be sure Herodotus actually saw a body being mummified – would mummymakers have wanted to reveal the tricks of their trade to a stranger? However, his depiction of the main stages – washing, drying out, and wrapping – seems fairly accurate.

In Egypt's, hot, fly-infested climate, relatives probably wasted no time in carrying their dearly departed to the tents of the *Ibu*,[2] or 'Place of Washing'. Here the body was stripped and cleaned in holy Nile water mixed with natron. The cleansed body was then carried to the another tent, known as the *Wabet*, 'the Pure Place'.

Here a team of priests treated and wrapped the body. Embalming a body was a holy act, as it attempted to recreate the rebirth of the first mummy, the god Osiris. As well as knowing their way around the inside of the human body, the priests needed to say the right prayer or spell at each stage of the process.

2. *The* Ibu *was in the desert, close to the burial ground but far from town, as the stench of rotting corpses could turn even the strongest stomach.*

Meet the Team

- **Overseer of Mysteries** (*hery seshta*). The chief embalmer. He dressed as Anubis, the god of mummification, and wore a large (scary) jackal mask. He chose the piece of linen that covered the mummy's head.

- **God's Seal Bearer** (*hetemu netjer*). The second in command, he had an ancient title dating from the 1st Dynasty.

- **The Lector Priest** (*hery heb*). This priest read the magic spells during each ritual.

- **Bandagers** (*wetyu*). They did most of the messy jobs (such as removing internal organs) and wrapped the body. At least they never got any complaints from their customers.

- **The Scribe** (*sesh*). He marked the line where the body was to be cut.

- **The Ripper** (*parascites*). Using a knife made from a sharp volcanic glass called obsidian, the 'Ripper' slit the body to remove the organs. After making his cut he was forced to flee as his fellow priests hurled ritual curses and even stones at him.

- Other priests organised the transportation and burial of the body.

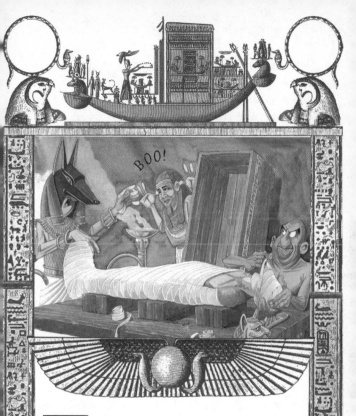

After a prank like this, Akil would have been scared stiff... if he wasn't stiff already!

The first job was to remove the brain. A small bronze rod was used to break the bone at the root of the nose. This made room for a hook or rod that was used to skewer the brain and  yank it out. Bits and pieces of grey matter were also scooped out with a long-handled spoon. Crafty undertakers may have pumped water into the brain, to make it rot quickly. Then they propped up the head and – *voilà!* – the liquid brain just oozed out of the nose. Hot liquid resin was then injected into the skull. When it set, any remaining spaces were packed with cloth and sawdust.

Jafari the embalmer gave a new meaning to the phrase 'pick your brains'.

A priest called the Ripper made a cut on the left side of the body and the internal organs were removed, including the lungs, stomach, intestines and liver.[3] The rib cage was then cut open to remove the lungs and to allow the mummymakers to clean the chest cavity. The heart was left in the body because it was thought to be responsible for thought, memory and intelligence. The mummy needed it to be judged in the next world, so if it got cut out by mistake it was quickly sewn back into place. The brain, meanwhile, was just thrown away!

The Egyptians believed that in the afterlife the body would become whole again, just like the god Osiris' had. After all the organs had been removed, the body was washed with wine and rubbed with sweet-smelling herbs and spices, before being packed with temporary stuffing material.

3. *Kidneys were often left in place, perhaps because they weren't considered important. In later times, the heart was also taken out, embalmed and replaced by a stone scarab (beetle) amulet, a symbol of rebirth.*

The Embalmer's Toolkit

- **Tools** – such as lamps, hooks, knives and pots.

- **Natron** – the natural salt used to dry the mummy's body, collected from the shores of desert lakes such as Wadi Natrun.

- **Table** – once at the 'Place of Washing', the body was placed on four wooden blocks resting on a low wooden table – embalmers usually worked while squatting. Tables were often soaked with natron and oils to help the drying and preserving process.

- **Incense** – this fragrant offering to the gods also had the added effect of making the terrible stench of the **festering** corpse just about bearable.

Take a deep bath in natron and feel the relaxing effects for over 3,000 YEARS!

- **Sawdust, sand, rags, straw** – all handy for stuffing/padding the body.

- **Frankincense and Myrrh** – these resins were rubbed onto mummies to make them smell nice.

- **Resin** – a sticky substance that trickles from the bark of fir and pine trees. When melted it was used to fill the mummy's head and body cavities and to coat coffins. It also smelt good.

- **Oil** – a scented oil (probably from juniper trees) used to massage the body. It was also applied to the wrapped corpse. King Tutankhamun's body was caked in oil and had to be cut out of the coffin by Egyptologist Howard Carter with a hot knife.

- **Palm wine** – may have been used to wash out the body as it is naturally antiseptic (stops bacteria from spreading).

- **Beeswax** – used to cover mouth and nostrils. The Egyptians believed bees were magical insects.

- **Onions** – used to fill in head and for false eyes. Also naturally antiseptic.

- **Coloured powders** – make-up for colouring the mummy.

Dried, Stuffed and Wrapped

After being emptied of all its internal organs, the corpse was placed on a sloping board and piles of solid natron were heaped in and around the body to dry it inside and out. Surrounded by scorching deserts, it seems odd that the mummymakers needed chemicals to dry out the body. But leaving hundreds of dead bodies out in the desert could have led to some embarrassing mix-ups. As the body slowly dried, the mummymakers got to work on the organs. They coated them in hot resin then wrapped them in the finest linen. The organs were then placed in four jars. By the 18th Dynasty, beautiful stone or pottery vessels were used, known today as canopic jars. Each lid represented one of the four sons of the god Horus, who were linked with the four points of the compass:

- **Imset**, a human, guarded the liver.
- **Hapy** the baboon protected the lungs.
- **Qebehsenuf** the hawk watched over the intestines.
- **Duamutef** the jackal guarded the stomach.

68

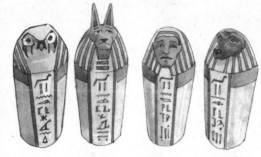

Qebehsenuf   Duamutef   Imset   Hapy

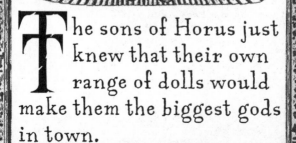

The sons of Horus just knew that their own range of dolls would make them the biggest gods in town.

Ooops!

Not all embalmers could be relied on to do a good job:

- The mummy of an official called Wah was found with the grubby embalmer's fingerprints inside his bandages, along with the remains of lizards, crickets and a mouse.

- Poor King Amenhotep III's face was twisted into a horrible grimace by resin stuffing which went hard.

- Princess Henttawi's mummified face was stuffed so full that her cheeks exploded, though she has since been restored. Her hair is made of string rather than real hair.

- One mummy from western Thebes was mummified upside down by muddled embalmers who added stuffing to the back of the head, body and limbs to give the appearance of a nose, chest and knees.

- Some embalmers cheated by breaking the bones to shorten the body, before throwing away the unwanted pieces.

- After the 22nd Dynasty, standards seem to have slipped. Mummymakers began to use less stuffing and more resin, which turned the mummies dark and heavy. X-rays have revealed that some mummies from this period are a jumble of bones, pottery, wood and other scrap materials!

- Old coffins were often reused to save money: one coffin from around 800 BC, which was originally painted with a pink face for a woman, was mistakenly used to hold a male official.

Princess Henttawi's make-up job left her cracking up!

After being dried in the bed of natron salt for 40 days, the body was then washed and all traces of the salt removed. The corpse was then taken to *Per-Nefer*, 'the House of Beauty', to be stuffed and shaped back to its normal size. The temporary stuffing was removed and replaced with resin-soaked linen and bags of sawdust or natron crystals, along with sweet-smelling spices such as myrrh, cinnamon and cassia.

The heart was also put back in place and the abdomen was then stitched up. At this point, the mummy looked a fright. Removing all the liquids from the body made it much lighter in weight and darker in colour.[4] The mummy's limbs were also skinny compared to the overstuffed body, and the face now looked shrivelled like a prune. Slits were cut in the shoulder and inside the mouth to allow the mummymakers to pad out the limbs and face.

4. The average human body has enough water to fill most of a 40-litre tank and enough fat to make seven bars of soap.

Badru always said he
had an eye for good
embalming.

Many perfumes and oils were rubbed on the body to smooth the skin and stop it from cracking, while the various cuts and slits were filled and covered with wax. Over the wax, a metal plate was glued into place to seal the wounds. This was carved with the Eye of Horus (*wedjat*) as, according to Egyptian myth, the god Horus had his eye magically restored after losing it in a battle with the evil god Seth. This protective symbol 'healed' the gash for the next life. As natron salt often made the finger and toe nails fall off, string was used to tie the nails on.

The Eye of Horus, or 'wedjat'

The Egyptians believed that a dead person's *Akh* had to return to the tomb and recognise its body before the mummy could live forever, so great care was taken to make the face look as good as possible. Cosmetics were used to draw lines to strengthen the eyebrows and mark the hairline. False plaits and curls were woven into the natural hair to make it look more lifelike. However, the bleached blonde hair on one mummy was probably a chemical reaction rather than a final flourish by the hairdresser.

As the eyeballs always rotted, they were shoved down into their sockets and replaced with fake eyes. While semi-precious stones and linen balls were often used, Ramesses IV's mummy was given small onions. The mummy of Ramesses II had peppercorns shoved in its nose to retain its distinctive hooked shape.

Linen and onions were also used to block the nostrils, while the tongue was covered with a sheet of gold. The whole mummy was often painted with a natural dye, ochre: men in red and women in yellow. **Henna** dye was also used as make-up, and wigs were added to

complete the look. The body was then coated with a layer of hot resin. Now stuffed, coloured and sealed against the damp, it was ready to be wrapped.

Wrapping the mummy took another 15 days. This was an expensive business. Although the linen bandages were made from a local crop, flax, it took some 375 square metres of the finest linen for a complete wrap.[5] Relatives donated cloth to the mummymakers and, in many cases, special fine cloth with spells written upon it was used. Poorer relatives handed over linen strips, perhaps torn from clothes the dead person had worn in life. One mummy was found wrapped up in a square sail complete with rigging loops.

5. There were around 20 alternating layers of bandages and shrouds on each mummy. Mummies were often wrapped in seven shrouds, as seven was believed to be a magic number.

Spare Parts

It was vital that nothing was missing on the voyage to the Otherworld. If a jackal ran off with a body part, mummymakers would make a replacement. Examples include:

- False wooden legs.

- Hair extensions – balding women had false hair woven into their locks.

- Artificial eyebrows.

- One mummy had leather patches to cover nasty bed sores.

- If a missing hair got into the wrong hands it could be magically used against the mummy, so all the dead person's hair was carefully laid in the tomb next to the body.

- If the real heart was damaged, an amulet of a scarab could act as a stand-in during the weighing ceremony by Anubis.

- In one instance, when embalmers had lost a woman's organs, they made false intestines from rope, a liver from cowskin and other organs from leather and rags.

After the corpse had been covered in a yellow burial sheet, or shroud, the wrapping began. Embalmers got to work on individual fingers and toes first, before wrapping the limbs. Wealthy mummies had golden sheaths, known as stalls, placed over the ends of the fingers and toes. The mummymakers then bandaged the head in a figure of eight before working their way down the body. While horror films often show mummies with their arms crossed over their chest, it was more common for the arms to be placed along the body, with the hands along the thighs.

As each body part was wrapped, magic spells were recited to protect the corpse in the afterlife. The linen bandages were constantly brushed with hot resin. This stuck them together and made them stiffen as they dried. Now tightly wrapped from head to foot, the mummy was covered in red shrouds, with spells painted onto the outer shroud.

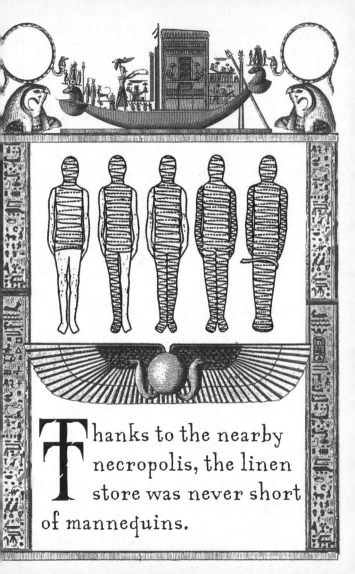

T hanks to the nearby necropolis, the linen store was never short of mannequins.

final Touches

Once the mummy was all wrapped up, a mask made of papyrus or linen and strengthened with plaster was then attached to the face using more bandages. The Egyptians believed that this would help the *Ka* and *Ba* identify the body if the real head was lost or damaged after burial. Royal mummies, such as Tutankhamun's, had highly decorated masks made of gold which were inlaid with precious stones. Magic spells were written on the shoulders and back to give the dead person the face of a god – or rather, the best bits of various different gods.

Tutankhamun's death mask, complete with false beard, vulture and cobra symbols.

As the Egyptians believed that the sun god Re had flesh made of pure gold, the body of a dead pharaoh was covered in gold. King Tutankhamun seems to have been very fond of earrings and his feet were tucked into solid gold sandals. A mummy could never have enough magical protection, so embalmers also hid jewellery and amulets between every layer of bandages.[6] Unfortunately, these treasures were also the reason why mummies were ripped apart or burnt by grave robbers.

When the mummy was packaged and ready for the afterlife, a priest recited a final prayer:

Hail Osiris, I shall possess my body for ever.
I won't come apart nor be eaten by worms.
I exist. I am alive...
My body will not be destroyed in the afterlife.

As the mummy was laid in the coffin, flower wreaths were hung around its neck.

6. While ordinary mummies had 40 or so amulets, Tutankhamun had an astonishing 140 amulets scattered through his wrappings.

81

Pick Your Charm

- **ankh** – the symbol of eternal life.

- **djed** – the pillar representing the backbone of Osiris: a symbol of strength and stability.

- **tet** – this charm protected the limbs.

- **winged scarab** – a symbol of rebirth, usually placed over the chest.

- **shen** – a circle of cord, to keep the body whole after death.

- **khefa** – the clenched fist gave you power and vigour in the afterlife.

- **bes** – this cheeky-looking dwarf god protected women and children.

- **head disc** – this was placed under the head with a spell to keep the head warm.

Scarab

Ankh

Seventy days after it was delivered to the 'Pure Place', the body was returned to the relatives along with the canopic jars and a whopping bill!

The whole process was done in secret, so the relatives had little or no way of knowing if they had been given back the right body. Meanwhile all the materials which were used to turn the body into a mummy were stored in large pots. They couldn't be thrown away as there was always the chance that they contained a bit of dead skin or a rotting fingernail that had dropped off. Around the same time, a large team of craftsmen and artists worked frantically to apply the finishing touches to the tomb in time for the funeral.

Embalming Tools

Coffins and Sarcophagi

After all the trouble taken to preserve the body, it made sense to use the very best coffin to preserve the body and to protect it from wild animals and (hopefully) tomb raiders. Made of wood, metal or pottery, coffins changed in style and decoration over time. In the Old Kingdom, kings and nobles were buried in plain coffins of cedarwood shipped from Byblos. By the Middle Kingdom, royal mummies were placed in a large stone container, called a sarcophagus.[7] Weighing up to 5 tonnes, it would have taken blood, sweat and tears to shift the block into position.[8]

Under the lid of the sarcophagus, two or more coffins were stacked inside each other like Russian dolls. The more important a person, the more coffins they had to write magic spells on. In the 18th Dynasty, King Tutankhamun had three human-shaped coffins, one of which

7. The word 'sarcophagus' means 'flesh eater'. The ancient Greeks, who coined the phrase, believed the body would be eaten away by the stone.
8. The black granite sarcophagus used by one of the last Egyptian pharaohs, Nectanebo I (who lived at the time of Alexander the Great), ended up in Alexandria and was used as a bathtub!

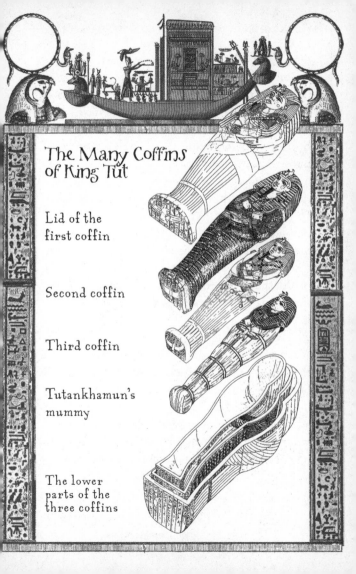

The Many Coffins of King Tut

Lid of the first coffin

Second coffin

Third coffin

Tutankhamun's mummy

The lower parts of the three coffins

was solid gold. These were inside a stone sarcophagus, which in turn had been placed inside four shrines, each made of wood covered in gold. From the 22nd Dynasty (9th century BC) the second coffin was replaced by a container made of plastered layers of papyrus or linen – a bit like heavy papier mâché. Known as *cartonnage*, this layer was decorated with colourful designs and gold. In the New Kingdom, most coffins were painted in bright cheerful designs showing magic symbols and scenes from *The Book of the Dead*. However, the Egyptian craftsmen who made these coffins didn't see them as art – they were magical objects that helped the dead live again.[9]

Mummies were often buried facing east so that they would face the rising sun. A pair of false eyes were painted on the coffin to allow a mummy to 'look out', and a painted door allowed the mummy's spirit to leave and re-enter the coffin as it wished. Tucked away in its nest of coffins, the mummy was now ready to enter the tomb, its home for eternity.

9. *The Egyptian word for the inner coffin,* suhet, *was also the word for 'egg', from which new life emerges.*

Under God's Wings

During the Second Intermediate Period (between the Middle and New Kingdoms), coffins took on a more human shape. Some had lids which were decorated with vulture wings. Known as *rishi* coffins (from the Arabic meaning 'feather'), the wings were either painted on or plastered and covered in gold. They represented the protective wings of gods and goddesses such as Horus and Isis.

Some coffin-makers put heart and soul into their products. Then again, so did the owners.

Animal Mummies

Eternity sounds like a very long time, but at least the Egyptians got to share it with their favourite pet! To them, it was only natural that humans and animals shared the afterlife together. American archaeologist Theodore Davis got a nasty fright when he entered one tomb in the early 1900s: in the dim light of the tomb he saw a large yellow dog with its tail curled over its back, staring at him, while sitting in front was a monkey. In fact, they were both mummies that had been unwrapped by ancient robbers and posed like this as a joke!

Animals were made into mummies for several different reasons: as pets for the dead, as offerings to gods, and as dinner for the dead person. Joints of meat and birds were mummified and brushed with hot resin for a 'just-roasted' appearance! The Ancient Egyptians loved their pets and some were given a funeral of their own. It wasn't just cats and dogs, though: King Amenhotep had a pet cemetery close to his own tomb containing a dog, five monkeys, a baboon, three ducks and an **ibis**. In 2003, the body of a mummified lion was found in the tomb of Tutankhamun's nurse,[10] while Princess Istemkheb had her cuddly pet gazelle buried with her.

Most Egyptian gods and goddesses were linked with animals: Thoth the scribe god appears as a baboon or an ibis; Amun could be a goose or a ram; while the goddess Wadjet was associated with cobras, lions, shrews and an Egyptian mongoose known as an ichneumon. Some gods had features of more than one animal: Opet, the mother goddess, was a hippo with a crocodile's tail.

10. *The lion could have been a pet – we know that Ramesses the Great had a pet lion named 'Slayer of my Enemies'.*

Some animals were even seen as living gods. The famous Apis Bull had his own temple at Memphis. To Egyptians, he was the living form of the god Ptah. When the bull died, Ptah's spirit jumped into another bull. Newborn calves all over Egypt were carefully examined to find one with exactly the right markings on its coat, tail and tongue.[11]

During festivals, eager worshippers asked the all-knowing Apis Bull for advice and priests explained its answers. When it died, the bull was mummified and buried in a giant stone sarcophagus. Two complete mummies have been found in a special tomb for bulls built by Ramesses II. The Egyptians also believed that bulls helped protect and guide the dead in the afterlife.

The Egyptians lived in awe of the fearsome crocodiles that lived along the Nile. They were linked with the mighty Sobek, the crocodile god worshipped in the temple at Kom Ombo (this bend in the river was a favourite spot for

11. The Greek historian Herodotus describes several of these special marks, such as a white square on the Apis Bull's forehead and the image of an eagle on its back.

crocodiles to bask in the sun). Here priests kept tame crocodiles as sacred pets, feeding them fine meats and wine and dressing them in gold earrings and bracelets. When they died, these sacred animals were mummified. Baby crocodiles and eggs were also sold to the public as offerings to Sobek.

From about 1000 BC, animal mummies became a big money-spinner for the temples. Millions of mummies were sold by the priests to worshippers, who left them at temples as a gift to the gods.[12] Mummies were often fakes containing mud, straw and odd bones. One crocodile mummy, once the pride of Leiden Museum in Germany, turned out to be two small mammals shoved end to end! This thriving industry meant that some temples became zoos. While the Temple of Bastet at Bubastis reared cats, the temple of Thoth at Hermopolis had hundreds of baboons and thousands of ibises wandering around.

12. Millions of ibis mummies found at Saqqara were offered to Imhotep, the human architect of the first pyramid. In time he was worshipped as a god of healing and the birds were offered to him by sick people hoping to be cured.

Khai would never know that they had made a monkey out of him!

Top Mummified Animals

X-rays reveal many interesting things about mummified animals. Dogs and cats were often mummified with great care and buried with the things they would need in the afterlife. Other animals, such  as crocodiles, were simply dipped in bitumen or resin. Animals given as offerings often had broken necks or battered skulls, so we know that they were deliberately killed.

- **Rams** – Though most rams died of old age, bone studies show that they were probably kept in a dark, narrow space, locked inside the temple.

- **Dogs** – Many of the dog mummies found at the necropolis at Asyut were strangled to death as a sacrifice to the god Anubis.

- **Baboons** – X-rays show that the mummy of a baby buried with its mother was actually a baboon. Was this a mix up at the mummymakers'?

(continued overleaf)

More Animal Mummies

- **Bulls** – X-rays show that some mummies contain just the bull's head and its bones. The body may have been cooked and eaten by the pharaoh before the bull was buried. Perhaps the Egyptians believed that eating the god gave him the bull's powers, as described in the famous 'Cannibal Hymn' in the *Pyramid Texts*.

- **Cats** – At the Temple of Bastet in Bubastis, visitors picked out a cat which the priest then killed by breaking its neck. The poor moggy was then mummified and, for a fee, buried in a local catacomb (underground tomb).

- **Snakes** – Cobras have been found mummified and wrapped up in small packets.

- **Crocodiles** – Crocodiles of different sizes could be wrapped together in a pile. Many crocodiles also had their snouts cut off and glass eyes (yellow with black pupils) put in place.

- **Birds** – Falcon mummies were buried with mummified shrews to feed them in the afterlife. Bird and reptile eggs were also mummified.

- **Shrews** – A shrew mummy was found placed inside a bronze case with a statue of a shrew on top.

CHAPTER THREE

TOMBS
A FINAL RESTING PLACE

The funeral

When the mummy was ready for burial, the coffin was placed on a funeral sledge, or **bier**. This was hauled by oxen to the bank of the Nile before being ferried across to the Western Desert. The Egyptians believed that as the sun set in the west, the dead came up from their tombs and looked back across the river at the land of the living. Long journeys were best done by boat, so being ferried across the Nile seemed a natural way to travel to the afterlife. Models of boats were often placed in the tomb to help the mummy continue its voyage through the Otherworld.

They all agreed it was a good mourning for a funeral procession.

The coffin, covered by a large canopy, was followed by priests, mourners dressed in white, a second bier carrying the canopic jars, a statue of the dead person, and servants bearing grave goods and offerings. The long procession was led by someone called the Sem priest, who wore a leopard's skin. This role was often performed by the dead person's male heir, or by the new pharaoh during royal funerals.

To purify the route, the Sem priest scattered milk on the ground in front of the bier. The route was lined with female mourners, either family members or women hired for the day. To show their grief, they tore their clothes, poured ash on their heads and wailed loudly as they raised their arms to the heavens. Royal funerals picked their way through the stacks of royal goods that were brought from palaces all over Egypt.

At the tomb, the Sem priest sprinkled water and burned sweet-smelling incense in front of the mummy. He then conducted the all-important Opening of the Mouth ceremony in the doorway of the tomb. The mummy was propped up and the Sem priest touched its mouth, eyes, ears, nose and other body parts using sacred objects.[1] At the same time he recited the spells that would give the mummy the power to speak, hear, see, taste and touch in the afterlife.

The Opening of the Mouth ceremony was followed by a banquet for the funeral party, who were entertained by dancers and musicians. Food was set aside for the mummy, as the Egyptians believed its *Ka* joined in the feast. The corpse was finally ready to be placed in the tomb. Every tomb had two parts. The first, below ground, was a store for the body that was sealed for eternity. Above ground was a chamber where the living brought offerings of food and water to feed the dead person's *Ka* in the afterlife.

---

1. *These included a magic wand known as a* pesesh-kef, *an adze (a tool used for smoothing rough-cut wood) and the foreleg of an ox!*

Grave Goods

A mummy was buried with all the things its *Ka* would need in the afterlife. Though magic took care of most of their needs, the rich still took valuable objects into tombs. The richer the individual, the more things they packed into their storerooms.

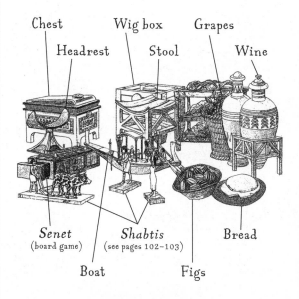

Chest

Headrest

Wig box

Stool

Grapes

Wine

Senet
(board game)

Shabtis
(see pages 102–103)

Boat

Figs

Bread

Ten Things to Take to the Grave
Don't get buried without them!

- **Model brewers** to brew beer in the afterlife

- **Harps** to play hymns to the gods

- **Board games**, such as *senet*, to while away eternity

- **Fans** made from ostrich feathers to keep you cool

- **Make-up** such as eye-liner so you look your best for the gods

- **Shoes** for padding around in the afterlife. Trendy King Tut had 100 pairs in his tomb!

- **First-aid kit**, just in case you trip and cut yourself in the afterlife

- **Chariot** for whizzing around in, although in a small tomb like Tutankhamun's the chariot had to be dismantled to fit it inside

- **Magic wands** to protect against poisonous snakes and scorpions in the afterlife

- **Food.** Early tombs were stockpiled with food for the Otherworld. The tomb of King Aha 'the Fighting Hawk' (1st Dynasty) in Abydos contained waterbirds, ox meat, bread, cheese, dried figs, jars of beer and wine vessels.

Once a year, the family and friends of the deceased celebrated his or her memory in the chamber outside the tomb. Special songs were composed just for the occasion. Those who couldn't afford to build a chamber held a picnic out in the open, known as a 'Feast of the Valley'. There was also the problem of feeding the *Ka* for eternity. Some families solved this by giving a plot of land to the cemetery priests to feed their dead relative. Others used magic: the right spells, models and pictures of what was needed in the afterlife could be a good substitute for the real thing.

The paintings in the tombs of ordinary men and women tell us a great deal about how the Egyptians lived: their family life, how they grew crops, brewed beer and built from wood and stone. To the deceased, the tomb painting was like a DVD of a perfect life that could be played over and over for eternity. The dead person was always shown as young and fit, perhaps because work on many tombs began while he or she was still young.

By contrast, royal tombs were decorated with holy images. The mummy of King Tutankhamun was surrounded by scenes mapping his journey to the afterlife and magic spells to help him on his way. The passageway leading to the burial chamber shows the 12 hours of night: the journey the dead pharaoh would have to make each night to ensure that the sun rose again the next day. One painting shows Tutankhamun travelling through the Otherworld on a boat marked by a scarab, the symbol of the sun god.[2]

Tomb magic had other uses, too. Pharaohs and nobles would need servants after death. During the Old Kingdom, servants were killed to accompany the king on his journey to the afterlife. By the Middle Kingdom, bloodshed was avoided as noble Egyptians had model servants known as *shabtis* placed in the tomb. Powerful spells brought *shabtis* to

2. The scenes painted on royal tombs also boasted (or rather, fibbed) about the pharaoh's achievements. King Pepi II's (6th Dynasty) mortuary temple is filled with carvings showing battles that had actually been won by King Sahure 200 years before. In Ramesses III's tomb, a painting shows him winning the Battle of Kadesh, even though it was fought 100 years earlier by his ancestor Ramesses II.

life, allowing them to answer the call of the gods if their master or mistress was asked to do a job in the afterlife.[3] Between 10 and 60 cm tall, *shabtis* were made of stone, wood, blue-glazed pottery and metal. They were often inscribed with the name and titles of the dead person they served.

Shabtis – ready to serve in the afterlife

3. The word shabti means 'the one who answers'. One spell in The Book of the Dead reads: "Oh Shabti, if your master is required to carry out a task in the Otherworld, you will say: Here I am!"

Human Sacrifice

In a recent archaeological dig, the bodies of six royal servants were found buried along with 1st-Dynasty King Aha. One of the children had ivory bracelets.

If that sounds bad, over 300 bodies were discovered around the tomb of his successor, King Djer. Surprisingly, human figures were also found in Djer's tomb, so perhaps even he realised the waste in sacrificing the living. By the end of the 1st Dynasty, the bloodthirsty practice had died out.

In the Middle Kingdom, two to five *shabtis* were placed in their own mini coffins. At first, they acted as substitutes for the main mummy if it got destroyed. Later on, *shabtis* appeared in groups, such as a squad of soldiers or a team of cooks. They held tools and weapons instead of being modelled with crossed arms. These *shabtis* were servants of the dead, and from the 18th Dynasty onwards, pharaohs couldn't have enough of them. King Tutankhamun was buried with 417 *shabtis*, while Seti I had more than 700. Some were stored in beautifully painted wooden boxes or pots.

from Pits to Pyramids

Just as paintings inside the burial chamber showed daily life, tombs were built to resemble houses of the living. Early tombs were very much like actual houses, such as the great underground palace built by the architect Imhotep for King Djoser (3rd Dynasty). The hundreds of tunnels around his burial chamber are like a small village – just like his royal palace.

The first tombs were just simple pits. Before the time of the pharaohs, chieftains were buried where they had been born or where they ruled. After King Narmer unified both Upper and Lower Egypt, tombs began to cluster around the royal burial site. In time, the mound of earth that covered the first pit graves was shaped more like a house. Brick steps protected an underground burial chamber below.

From the 1st Dynasty onwards (around 3500 BC) tombs got larger and more lavish: the royal tomb of King Wadj at Saqqara was 50 metres long and 15 metres wide. Known as *mastaba*, they were built from mud bricks in the shape of a long bench with a flat roof. The burial chambers, cut into the rock below, were connected to the surface by a long tunnel. The royal tomb was surrounded by smaller graves for nobles, workers and servants.

The first pyramid, built for King Djoser (3rd Dynasty) started out as a *mastaba*. The architect Imhotep changed the shape into a square, then built a smaller square on top. By adding four more square storeys, each smaller than the one before, he created the Step Pyramid, the first large stone monument in the world. The tomb is just as impressive below ground: there are more than 5.5 kilometres of tunnels and a 27-metre shaft leads to the burial chamber. Everything in the tomb is made from stone: copies of wooden doors, metal pots, and straw baskets. Imhotep had taken Djoser's home and turned it into stone – so it would last for ever.

The Step Pyramid – the first ever 'Stairway to Heaven'.

The earliest smooth-sided pyramid, at Meidum, started out as a step pyramid, though later monuments, such as the Bent Pyramid and Red Pyramid at Dahshur, were designed with smooth sides from the outset. To the Egyptians, step pyramids were a stairway to heaven that allowed the pharaoh to join the sun god Re. By the 4th dynasty, Egyptian craftsmen had learned to cut and polish hard stone such as granite and basalt, which they used to build corridors and protect the burial chamber.

During the Old and Middle Kingdoms (2628–1638 BC), most Egyptian kings were buried in pyramids, while nobles were still buried in underground chambers below *mastabas*. Members of the royal family had their own burial chambers, each with its own shaft, and a chapel was built into each pyramid so that offerings could be made.

Pyramid Rituals

The priests who worked in the mortuary temple attached to each pyramid had a busy daily schedule (in theory their job lasted for eternity). They were divided into groups of 10, with each group on duty for a month.

- After opening the shrine they removed the linen shawl on the statue of the pharaoh inside the temple. The statue was then washed and given a fresh shawl while one priest recited sacred prayers and another wafted sweet-smelling incense around the room.

- A ritual meal was placed before the false door between the offering hall and the pyramid. It was later given to retired priests to feed them.

- Sacred water was poured on the offering table. This flowed into a basin which was then emptied into a channel leading under the wall of the offering hall and into the main pyramid.

- Twice a day, two priests would walk around the pyramid in a clockwise direction, sprinkling it with sacred water.

- At the end of the ceremony, all the equipment was checked for the next day.

An example of a fairly simple pyramid design – one for the amateur tomb raider.

Some 50 royal pyramids were built, though most are smaller than the awesome pyramids of the 4th-Dynasty rulers Khufu, Khafre and Menkaure.

Khufu's pyramid alone weighs 6.5 million tons and is 146 metres tall. By the 5th-Dynasty, the pyramids were decorated on the inside. These hieroglyphic writings, the aforementioned *Pyramid Texts*, are the earliest versions of the spells that ensured a safe voyage to the Otherworld.

By the 11th dynasty, tombs were cut into solid rock up to 2 km from the pyramid or chapel. To outwit tomb robbers, corridors were designed with sharp turns, dummy passageways and trap doors.

The Valley of the Kings

In the New Kingdom, the pharaohs built their tombs in the Valley of the Kings[4] at Thebes (across the river from the modern town of Luxor). Hidden behind a group of hills, the Valley is quite close to the river Nile. The high cliffs that surround it offer a natural defence against tomb robbers. The only pyramid in sight is the mountain El-Qurn, which towers over the valley.

Underground tombs were now the norm; long passages led to a series of chambers cut deep into the rock. Unlike the bare walls inside the great pyramids, these tombs were decorated with brightly coloured scenes from *The Book of the Dead* and the journey through the Otherworld. They became more and more elaborate as their architects and artists experimented with different styles.

---

4. *The Egyptians called the Valley of the Kings 'The Great and Majestic Necropolis of the Millions of Years of the Pharaoh, Life, Strength, Health in The West of Thebes', or, if they were in a hurry, 'The Great Place'.*

Merneptah's tomb was the first to be cut straight from the door down to the tomb with no sudden turns to block the daylight from the burial chamber. Seti I's tomb, over 120 metres deep, has two large chambers decorated with columns. His son Ramesses II built a giant underground labyrinth with over 100 chambers to house the bodies of around 50 of his sons when they died.

Cutaway view of an underground tomb

The Valley of the Kings also had tombs for pharaohs' wives and children and for favoured nobles and their families. At the time of Ramesses I (around 1300 BC), work started on the Valley of the Queens, although some wives were still buried with their husbands.

By the end of the New Kingdom, however, Egypt was in decline. The Valley was no longer a safe burial place for mummies. During the 21st Dynasty the priests of Amun opened most of the tombs and moved the mummies and their treasures to protect them from robbers. Pharaohs were now buried near the temple of Amun at Tanis, the northern capital. Compared to the opulent splendour of the former pharaohs' tombs, burial was cheap and cheerful. Older tombs and sarcophagi were recycled, and in some tombs dozens of coffins might be stacked together in a great heap.[5]

5. In 1891 a tomb was discovered at Bab el-Gasus measuring 155 metres long. Inside, French archaeologist Georges Daressy discovered 163 sets of coffins and mummies and 110 boxes of shabtis all buried together.

The Lost Labyrinth

During the 12th dynasty, the pharaohs reclaimed large areas of land in the marshy Faiyum region (southwest of Cairo), creating a giant lake known as Lake Moeris. Ammenemes III built his funeral temple nearby, known as the 'labyrinth'. Though it has never been found by modern archaeologists, Herodotus wrote that it was even more amazing than the pyramids. He named the building after the labyrinth of King Minos of Crete. In ancient Greek legend, King Minos' labyrinth was home to the Minotaur, a monster who was half-bull and half-man.

This gigantic tomb must have been some 300 metres long by 240 metres wide, with 3,000 rooms (half above ground and half below), linked by a maze of passages. Despite its size, perhaps it still lies hidden somewhere beneath the desert sands...

Tomb Workers

Though Ancient Egyptian artists didn't sign their works, we know about the architect Imhotep. Creator of the Step Pyramid, in Egyptian legend he was the first person to build in stone. Bak was chief sculptor in the reign of Akhenaten (18th-Dynasty), while the sculptor Tuthmosis may well have carved the famous bust of Akhenaten's wife Nefertiti, which now resides in the Egyptian Museum, Berlin.

Some of the artists at work in the Valley of the Kings are also known, such as the scribe Ramose and the **foreman** Kaha. While the great pyramids were probably built by huge gangs of 20,000 or so workers during the flood season, smaller tombs could be cut into the rock by a much smaller group of skilled labourers. Known as the 'Servants in the Place of Truth', they lived in an isolated desert village, now known by its Arabic name Deir el-Medina, a purpose-built complex where they enjoyed special privileges.

All of the artists belonged to a guild and had a workplace which they could pass on to family members or sell. The workers were split into two gangs from the east and west sides of Deir el-Medina. Each team had a scribe who wrote down what work was done and checked that the correct wages were paid. If the vizier (an important official in charge of building the tomb) was pleased with their progress, the workers might receive extra rations.

Teams of up to 120 men would work for eight days in the Valley of the Kings, then walk the 3 kilometres home for the ninth and tenth days, their 'weekend'. In their spare time, the workmen also built tombs for themselves. Servants did their washing and shopping to give the craftsmen more time to work on the royal tomb.

Seven Steps to Building a Tomb

Building the pharaoh's tomb was a huge project that took great skill – and a lot of patience. The vizier visited the tomb regularly to check on the work.

1. A site was chosen after studying plans of previous tombs – to avoid cutting into them. Scribes jotted notes down on flat flakes of stone they found lying outside the tomb.

2. A foundation ceremony was held at the site. Ritual objects were buried in a small pit in front of the proposed entrance.

3. After the surface sand was removed, the tunnelling began.

4. The entrance was hollowed out, then steps were cut down to the burial chambers and storerooms. Blocks cut from the cliff were huge and had to be split up before they could be removed.

5. The tunnels plunged deeper and deeper, down to a level where the pharaoh's body was to lie. In some rooms pillars of rock were left standing to support the ceiling. Labourers worked by the light from hundreds of oil lamps. Porters carried the rubble to the surface.

6. Plasterers smoothed the walls ready for decoration. Ceilings and floors were polished with rough stones.

7. The tomb was decorated. Some carvings were done in wet plaster, whereas others were cut directly into the hard rock. Artists working in teams then painted the various scenes (working from sketches done on flakes of rock).

PS. You never knew when a pharaoh was going to die: sometimes a storeroom had to be hastily converted into a burial chamber at the last minute!

In its heyday, the Valley of the Kings buzzed with activity as over 100 quarrymen, stonemasons, scaffolders, plasterers and artists went to work. **Coppersmiths** worked flat out to provide the **masons** with copper blades for their chisels (iron and bronze tools weren't yet used). Limestone is a relatively easy rock to cut, but many tombs had a steep entrance and the labourers would have sweated to carry the leather baskets of rubble to the surface. They were supplied by a continuous line of donkeys bringing food and water.

Building a royal tomb cost a fortune: expeditions were sent far and wide to bring back stone that would protect the dead pharaohs for eternity[6] – or so they hoped. The pharaohs of the 19th Dynasty were so confident about security in the Valley that they didn't even bother to hide the doorways to their tombs.[7] Big mistake. Of the 23 royal tombs in the Valley, only one, that of King Tutankhamun, kept its treasure until modern times.

Even in the afterlife, young Tutankhamun was an expert player of hide-and-seek.

6. Hard stones came from Gebel Ahmar, near Cairo, red granite came from Aswan, and soft stones, such as travertine, were found along the Nile. The Egyptians didn't care much for marble, though they could have used it, as there were good quarries in the Eastern Desert.
7. Though the tomb of Ramesses II was protected by a wooden door, this was easily smashed down by robbers.

WAKING THE DEAD

Torchlight Robbery

It took a huge amount of effort (and a large chunk of money) to mummify a body and to provide it with a tomb built for eternity. Sadly, most of ancient Egypt's royal graves were looted in ancient times, many shortly after they were sealed. For what grave robber could resist the lure of the golden treasures and glittering jewels buried within the dead pharaohs?

Despite the ever-present threat from police patrols, generations of robbers hid among the desert hills until dark, then sneaked down to plunder the tombs. Once inside the tomb, the thieves usually made a beeline for the mummy. They had all the time in the world to lever the lid off the sarcophagus or simply smash it to pieces. Heavy coffins provided no defence, even though some were fitted with cunning locks. Once the body was uncovered, mummies were often hacked to pieces in the search for the amulets which were easy to hide and sell on.

Robbers had few qualms about disturbing the dead. The mummy of 19th-Dynasty King Siptah was badly mangled by robbers, who also lopped the gold from the top of his coffin.[1] Thieves in another tomb even used the mummified children buried there as a torch to light the pitch-black burial chamber.

1. It was later repaired by 21st-Dynasty priests, who put Siptah's arm in a splint before rewrapping him. They also repaired his coffin (which originally had belonged to a woman), writing the king's names and titles over the damaged areas.

At long last, Mudada's collection of extremely rare *shabti* brewers was complete!

Heads, You Lose!

Be they for the rich or for the poor, few tombs escaped the **scourge** of the tomb robbers. If thieves came across pit graves in the desert sands, they dug down until they found the mummy's head. As they yanked it up to the surface, arms, legs and other body parts often got left behind.

The best defence against robbers was to hide the tombs – a large pyramid in the middle of a flat plain is much easier to spot than holes tucked away in a cliff face. During the Old Kingdom, the tomb builders tried all sorts of tactics. Most were very simple. False tombs, sometimes with a small stash of treasure to fool the robbers, were built in obvious locations, while the actual tombs were out in the desert, their entrances blocked with giant plugs of stone. Without dynamite or gunpowder, it would have taken a very patient robber to chip these away.

Egyptian tombs also contained a variety of traps. These weren't built simply to alert others to a robbery. No, they were built to kill the intruders. Heavy rocks did a good job of crushing a robber's head: they were placed above doorways and connected to wires or ropes that could bring them tumbling down. For example, a human skeleton was found inside the pyramid of 4th-Dynasty Queen Khamerernebty II that was clearly not the queen's. Was this an unfortunate tomb robber who got trapped?

Hidden holes led to steep pits or wells below the tomb. Difficult to spot in the dark, these may have had false covers that would have collapsed as robbers crept over them. Tombs also contained twisting corridors that led to dead ends or false graves. The burial chamber in the tomb of Senusret I was protected by a series of stone slabs. The first slab, once lowered, could not be forced upwards again because bolts were released from holes in the slab, locking it. To spook thieves, mortuary priests may have spread the idea that the *Ka* of the dead person protected the grave.

However, all these tactics still dismally failed to stop the robbers. In the Middle Kingdom, a locking coffin was developed (to protect against theft by undertakers as much as grave robbers) and during the New Kingdom security was stepped up around the Valley of the Kings. From the 19th Dynasty all tomb workers had to live at Deir el-Medina. The village was surrounded by a thick wall and a single gateway led in and out, making it easy for security guards to frisk labourers for stolen items. There were only two approaches into the Valley itself, which had its own police force and was guarded by a fortress and a ring of security huts.

Hold Your Breath

When Egyptologist Zahi Hawass entered the tomb of a local mayor, Eyuf, in the so-called Valley of the Golden Mummies, one room was covered in a 60 cm layer of yellow powder that made his team sick. Was this a booby-trap to ward off unwelcome visitors?

Amenemhet's 'Super-Tomb'

The Hawara pyramid of Amenemhet III, located near the Faiyum oasis (southwest of Cairo), contained some of the most cunning anti-theft devices ever seen.

- The entrance led to a small chamber, connected to a passage that looked like a dead end. In the roof was a huge stone weighing over 22 tonnes.

- When the giant roof slab was slid sideways, it revealed another false passage. But a hidden brick door led to a third corridor. Two more sliding ceiling blocks finally led the way to the burial chamber.

- The burial chamber was a piece of technical wizardry. It was carved from a single piece of hard stone, so the only way in was through the roof. Before the roof was put in place, the king's sarcophagus was lowered into the burial chamber. Then sand holding up the roof was allowed to move into pits next to it, lowering the roof on top of the chamber and closing it.

Alas, these devices still weren't enough to stop Amenemhet's big sleep from being disturbed. Though the robbers got side-tracked tunnelling down false passages, in the end they mined their way into the burial chamber.

If the ancient Egyptians were so religious, why did they rob graves? Surely it would have ruined any chance of the mummies inside ever getting through the Otherworld! Thousands of years later, it's hard to know for sure. Tomb raiders may have been hard up and desperate,[2] or non-believers. When one judge asked a thief: 'Why did you steal from the pharaoh's tomb', he simply replied: 'If the pharaoh is a god, why didn't he stop me?'

Some historians believe that professional tomb robbers may have belonged to a sect that worshipped the 'evil' god Seth, who chopped up Osiris in the original myth of the first mummy. If so, they would have had no respect for mummies whatsoever. Others have suggested that tomb robbers, angry at the terrible state of affairs in Egypt, were simply taking revenge on dead pharaohs whose job it was to look after their people.

2. Tombs are still being pillaged today, so when a new tomb is found, everything inside is removed to a safe place. Any new royal tombs discovered in the future will probably have already been disturbed by robbers. Of course, to the Egyptians, archaeologists removing the treasures for study would have been considered as evil as those dastardly grave robbers.

The thought of all that gold lying around was probably just too tempting. The Egyptians believed that the flesh of the gods was made of gold, so priests surrounded a mummy with as much gold as the dead person's relatives could afford. Today we still marvel at the solid gold mask of King Tutankhamun, a young and relatively unimportant king. Imagine the treasures that would have been buried with a mighty pharaoh like Ramesses II!

Caught in the Act

If caught, tomb robbers were beaten and tortured by tomb inspectors. If found guilty, they would have been put to work in the mines or killed 'on the wood' – impaled on wooden spikes. If the mummy of a dead pharaoh had been attacked, inspectors were allowed to torture suspects by chopping off their ears, nose and other parts of their face.

Hieroglyph showing a tomb robber being impaled on a spike

Things didn't always go the robbers' way – in the necropolis at Riqqeh, the skeleton of a robber was found crushed by rocks. The tomb roof had collapsed just as he was snatching jewels from a mummy. There was also the danger of getting caught. A cloth rag found in Tutankhamun's tomb was wrapped around some gold rings. It was possibly dropped by thieves as they were being chased by guards.

Despite the dangers, robbery was clearly still worth it – a thief's share of the loot might be worth a year's pay or more. That said, it's wrong to think that all tomb robbers were scoundrels who enjoyed raiding the final resting places of Egyptians. It was okay for certain people to enter a tomb and remove objects for use in their own burials. Tutankhamun's second inner coffin, four of his miniature canopic coffins, and the golden bands around his mummy were all swiped from the grave goods of his older brother, Smenkhkare. Many later pharaohs were buried in recycled coffins or borrowed tombs, perhaps seeing themselves as sharing the tomb with the spirit of the original owner.

Whodunnit?

- **The Burial party** sealing the family vault might be tempted to help themselves. The beautiful outer coffin of the 21st-Dynasty Princess Maatkare seems untouched, but below the lid of her inner coffin the thick gold sheet that once covered her face and hands has been heaved off. Guests at her funeral would have been none the wiser as they watched the beautiful priestess being placed inside her tomb.

- **Embalmers** may have robbed the mummy of Princess Henttawi before her body even reached the tomb, as the family had no way of knowing what was underneath all those bandages.

- **Court officials** could be bribed to turn a blind eye to tomb robbing.

- **Tomb builders**, especially stonemasons, had the skills and the tools to crack open any tomb.

- **Labourers** digging a new shaft might stumble across an old tomb stuffed with loot.

- **Priests** in the 21st-Dynasty 'saved' the mummies of older pharaohs from robbers. Though they repaired damaged mummies, could they have resisted pinching any remaining jewels?

Stop, Thief!

Perhaps the best account of tomb-robbing comes from the 20th-Dynasty. Though the full story will never be known, we do have lists of suspects and stolen goods. At this time, several kings had died in quick succession. Tombs were left unfinished, and by the ninth year of Ramesses IX, rations were running short at Deir el-Medina. Meanwhile the region was under attack from Libyan raiders and bandits roaming the Nile valley. With the king and his army further north, the tomb builders were defenceless. The angry workmen went on strike, and the riot squad was sent in, led by the High Priest at Thebes.

With all this going on, it's no wonder that the royal tombs became a target. In one instance, three men were found acting suspiciously in an area where the King's relatives were buried. They were let off without any charge by the police, who were under the command of the mayor of West Thebes, named Paweraa. Hearing rumours, Paser, the mayor of East Thebes, accused Paweraa himself of tomb robbing.

At first, Paser got nowhere – Paweraa paid off the witnesses and rigged a local inquiry. Paweraa also tried to intimidate Paser by organising a protest outside Paser's house. In desperation, Paser appealed to Ramesses IX, who ordered a new investigation. Some 45 people were arrested and tortured, and eight men were eventually found guilty of stealing from King Sobekemsaf I's tomb (17th Dynasty). Thanks to papyrus records, we can read their confession today: 'We took our copper tools and forced a way into the pyramid of this king through its innermost part…'

It seems likely that the loot stolen from the tombs benefited the whole community at Deir el-Medina. In fact, most tombs were probably pillaged by the very priests and tomb workers who built them or laid the dead to rest. One of their tricks was to tunnel into the tomb from behind, so there was no evidence that a robbery had even taken place.

First on the shopping list were gold and silver, which could be melted down and swapped for oxen. Goods such as expensive oils, spices, and wine were also easy to sell on, as were the fine linens that the rich had buried with them. Some thieves simply set fire to the burial chambers, then returned hours later to scrape up the hardened pools of gold from the floor.

Court records show the thieves often worked in gangs of about seven or eight, including stonemasons to open the royal sarcophagus and blacksmiths to melt down the stolen metals in a furnace. On top of this, a boatman would be bribed to ferry the robbers across the Nile to sell their treasures. The gangs were well organised and well connected, so officials could be bribed to look the other way. Over time, the tomb robbings went from bad to worse. Soon just about every valuable tomb at Thebes was ransacked.

Ancient Wheeler-Dealer

One papyrus describes the crimes of chief workman Paneb, who was caught stealing from the tombs of Seti II and Henutmire, wife of Ramesses II. Paneb was also accused of attacking a woman, digging up tombs, attempted murder and sleeping with the wives of several of his workmen. He seems to have secured his job as chief workman by bribing the 19th-Dynasty vizier Preemheb with a gift of five servants. We don't know how the court case went – did he manage to bribe his way out of that as well?

Tomb robbery became an even greater problem after the pharaohs abandoned the Valley of the Kings. During the 21st-Dynasty, the priests of Amun were sent on a rescue mission to remove the royal mummies that had been violated by robbers and hide them where they could be better protected. First, the mummies were taken to two workshops in the temple of Ramesses III and the empty tomb of Ramesses IX in the Valley. In secret, the priests stripped the so-called 'wandering' mummies of their remaining gold and jewels, perhaps to deter future robbers. The mummies were then repaired and stored in temporary hiding places until they could be transferred to the Royal Cache (a hidden store). This secret tomb was cut in the rock close to Deir el-Bahri.

Examples of tomb treasures

Eating Mummy

In medieval Europe, scholars only knew about Egypt from the Bible and the writings of ancient geographers such as Herodotus and Diodorus Siculus. Despite this, the legends of mummies and their fabulous treasures were well known. By the 16th century, Europeans were increasingly obsessed with mummies, not for their history, but to use as medicines. Since at least AD 1000, people had been 'eating mummy' – burning mummies, grinding them up and turning them into a powder.[3] In the 12th century, returning Crusaders brought news of the healing powers of these ground-up mummy parts. In their desperation to find a cure for their illness, people forgot that they were being cannibals!

3. *This was due to the belief that mummies were covered in bitumen, as breathing in its fumes was once thought to be good for your health. One popular belief of the 16th century was that the mummified flesh of witches and redheads provided the best medicine!*

Mummy trafficking became widespread. One merchant, John Sanderson, bought 270 kg of mummified flesh to sell to the English market in the 1580s. Egyptian mummies were so in demand that a priest to Queen Catherine de Medici of France made a special expedition to Egypt in 1549. Joining forces with a group of doctors from Italy, he broke into several tombs around Saqqara to hunt for mummies. Catherine's father-in-law, King Francis I of France, carried ground-up mummy (mixed with crushed rhubarb) in a pouch, in case he was wounded while hunting.

The word 'mummy' appears in many medical texts of the time, including those of Francis Bacon, and it is one of the ingredients in the witches' brew in Shakespeare's *Macbeth*. King Charles II collected the dust that fell off mummies. He used it on his skin, believing the power of the ancient pharaohs would rub off. In 1694, the French pharmacist Pierre Pomet gave advice on buying good-quality mummy powder: "look for one that is black without bones or dust, with a nice smell of something burnt rather than tar or resin."

Scale of
dragon, tooth
of wolf and
witch's mummy –
far from yummy!

The Wonder Drug

Avicenna, a Persian doctor born in 980 AD, is often regarded as the father of modern medicine. Yet even he recommends powdered mummy as a cure for ailments such as:

- broken bones
- coughs
- stomach upsets
- being poisoned
- liver problems
- being knocked out
- and even fear of heights!

During the 17th century, European merchants created a thriving market for mummies. If they couldn't get their hands on the real thing, they could buy fake mummies from Arab businessmen who had started to make them from recently executed criminals and people who had died from disease. They stuffed the bodies with bitumen, wrapped them in linen and left them in the sun to dry. When they were dry enough to look like real mummies, the dealers sold the shrivelled flesh to gullible Europeans.

Shaken or Stirred?

Mummy was usually used as a powder but mummified bodies were also boiled to produce a tasty brew! According to the French surgeon Ambroise Paré, however, eating mummy gave patients some nasty side-effects: 'It causes great pain in their stomachs, gives them evil-smelling breath and brings about serious vomiting.'

LOOK AWAY!

There were several stories of supposedly ancient mummies being 'recognised' by their living relatives. Usually, however, there were plenty of dead bodies to go round: visitors to Saqqara in the 17th century report seeing corridors packed with thousands of mummies. Fears that fake mummies could spread disease, and a heavy tax on mummy flesh, finally put an end to the trade in the 18th century.

The first Tomb Explorers

Until the 18th century, most people's idea of Egypt was a mix of myth and fantasy, and early European explorers had no more respect for the dead pharaohs than their tomb-raiding Egyptian predecessors (though they were more interested in statues and carvings than jewels). One of the first to explore the ancient tombs was Italian former circus strongman Giovanni Battista Belzoni (1778–1823), who discovered the tombs of Ramesses I and Seti I in the Valley of the Kings, and of Khafre in the Second pyramid at Giza.

Everything in Egypt changed in 1798 with the arrival of French military leader Napoleon's troops. As the British Empire spread across Asia, Napoleon invaded Egypt to block Britain's eastern trade routes. He took with him a force of 328 ships and 40,000 men, including a team of 175 scholars with scientific instruments to record the monuments, geography and wildlife of Egypt.

Smash and Grab

Giovanni Belzoni had a great knack for discovering tombs, but he was more interested in finding treasure or papyri for his exhibition in London than looking at dead pharaohs. In one tomb he discovered, he sat down for a rest. The coffin he sat on crumbled beneath him and he sank into a dusty pile of bones, rags and dried flesh!

When Belzoni later stumbled on Khafre's sarcophagus inside the second pyramid at Giza, he scratched his name across the walls of the burial chamber. Show some respect!

Unlucky Dip!

According to the British Egyptologist E. A. Wallis Budge, in the early 1800s a group of gold-hunters came across a tomb with a mysterious sealed jar. Opening the jar, they found it contained honey. Feeling peckish, they began dipping their bread into it. Then one of them spotted a clump of hair in the honey. It got worse – pulling hard, out came the body of a tiny child that had been preserved in the honey!

Napoleon's scientific team mapped large areas of the country. The expedition travelled up the Nile as far as Aswan, taking note of many ancient monuments that have since disappeared. On its return to France, notes from the expedition were made into a book, *The Description of Egypt*, a classic guide to ancient Egypt. It contained many wonderful pictures that aroused a great interest in Egypt around the world.

144

Militarily, Napoleon's expedition was a disaster, and a lot of Egyptian material fell into British hands after the surrender of Alexandria. However, several mummies and coffins were shipped home by the French. Two detached heads were given to Napoleon and his wife Josephine as a present, while other mummies were displayed in the Louvre museum in Paris. When later the mummies started to rot, they had to be buried in the palace gardens.

In 1842, King Friedrich Wilhelm IV of Prussia asked Prussian explorer Richard Lepsius to lead an expedition to Egypt to explore and record the remains of the ancient Egyptian civilisation. Lepsius made detailed studies of the Valley of the Kings and around Giza (20 km southwest of Cairo), where he discovered over 67 pyramids and more than 130 noble tombs.[4] He later returned home with 15,000 items that he donated to the Berlin Museum.

---

4. *It was Lepsius who came up with the name for the scroll of spells written inside tombs* – The Book of the Dead.

The Rosetta Stone

In 1799, during the French expedition into Egypt, a discovery was made which would change our knowledge of Egypt forever: a 760 kg stone featuring three translations of a single piece of text. Two were Egyptian but one was classical Greek, making it possible for French scholar Jean-François Champollion (1790–1832) to decipher the Egyptian language in 1822. After thousands of years, scholars could once again read the inscriptions on statues, tomb walls and mummy cases.

Found at Rosetta, and now residing at the British Museum, this code-breaking stone is the key to our modern understanding of ancient Egyptian hieroglyphics.

Despite their scientific aim, these expeditions and collections sent people mummy-mad back in Europe. Wealthy tourists flocked to Egypt in droves during the first half of the 19th century, and many took mummies home with them as souvenirs of their visit. Back in Europe, mummy unwrapping parties were the height of fashion. The Victorians invited friends over to watch the bandages being peeled away, followed by refreshments. Amulets taken from the wrappings were sometimes given as trinkets to the guests, and the unwrapped mummy would be displayed in the house.

Some unwrappers had a serious interest in mummies, whereas others saw unwrappings as a way to make a quick buck. In 1834, Dr Thomas J. Pettigrew, also known as 'Mummy' Pettigrew, performed his first public mummy unwrapping in London's Royal College of Surgeons. For the next 20 years, he unwrapped mummy after mummy, always to packed houses – the Archbishop of Canterbury was once turned away from a sell-out performance.

Top Tips for Stealing a Mummy

- **Keep your eyes peeled.** When entering a burial chamber, make sure no-one is looking before yanking off a mummy's hands, feet, arms and head for your private collection. If you think you can get away with it, why not run off with a whole body?
- **Mummies stink.** Two ladies who had sneaked a mummy onto their houseboat couldn't put up with the terrible stench and were forced to heave it overboard.
- **Avoid the police.** One gentleman travelling across Europe with two mummies was almost arrested for being a murderer. The police thought he was trying to get rid of the bodies.
- **Beware of fakes.** A tourist who bought a mummy in Aswan later found out the body belonged to an English engineer who had died there recently.
- **Tourist scams.** Some tourist operators deliberately sowed ancient burial grounds with bodies shipped in from other sites. When English King Edward VII visited the 'opening' of one tomb and watched as a mummy was discovered inside, he didn't realise the whole show had been faked for his benefit. When the tomb had first been opened, 40 years before, it contained just an empty sarcophagus.
- **Travel by land.** The sarcophagus of 4th-Dynasty pharaoh Menkaure was lost in a shipwreck in the Mediterranean.

Digging for The Dead

For a long time, Egyptian mummies were seen as playthings to be dug up, sold and thrown away. Perhaps the first person to treat them as valuable historical objects was the Frenchman Auguste Mariette, who set up the Cairo Museum in 1863. He began the first official excavations and did everything he could to save Egyptian **antiquities**: he even forced his wife to hand over a scarab she had bought.

Even so, few mummies were studied or properly preserved and it was still easy enough to buy one and ship it home. More care was taken after the spectacular discovery of the mummies in the Royal Cache (hidden store) at Deir el-Bahri in 1881. Hearing that royal grave goods were on sale, Émile Brugsch, who worked for the Cairo Museum, tracked down the three Abd el-Rassul brothers from the notorious treasure-hunting village of Qurna. Under torture, they confessed that one brother, Ahmed, had found the tomb while looking for a lost goat.

Six Ways to Use a Mummy

- **Paint a picture.** An oil paint, called Mummy Brown, was manufactured from mummy parts up until the 20th century.

- **Wrap up sausages.** Augustus Sandwood, an American paper merchant, imported mummies to make rag paper from their bandages. These were too stained to make anything but brown wrapping paper, which Sandwood sold to butchers and grocers. When an outbreak of **cholera** was traced to his mill, the operation was shut down.

- **Use as ballast or fertiliser.** Cat mummies were used in ships to stop them tipping over in heavy seas. They were also used as fertiliser in England until a public outcry put an end to it.

- **Lighting.** Local Egyptians used pieces of mummies as fuel for fires or ripped off arms or legs and set them on fire to light their way in dark tombs.

- **Furniture.** In 1971, the Nieman Marcus department store in the United States offered 'his and hers' mummy cases for sale for $5000 in their catalogue. The coffins were bought by a museum, who found that one of them contained a mummy, a priest named Usermontu.

- **Eat it.** French king Louis XIV had his heart mummified when he died in 1715, but during the French Revolution, 75 years later, his tomb was ransacked by revolutionaries. Louis'  heart was stolen and was eventually bought by the Dean of Westminster (a high-ranking London clergyman), the Very Reverend William Buckland. The Dean, who liked to try new foods, had the heart sautéed, slow-roasted and served with a side of broad beans. He then ate the heart for Christmas supper. He noted that it was a little on the chewy side, but was otherwise very tasty!

Louis XIV, eat your heart out!

When he was shown the tomb, Émile Brugsch promptly hired 300 workmen, who cleared the cache in six days. The rescued royalty were loaded on board the Museum steamer and taken to Cairo to keep them safe from robbers. Brugsch and his brother later made an important find at Saqqara – the Old Kingdom spells used to protect the dead (now known as the *Pyramid Texts*). When they tried to remove one mummy from this site it broke in half, so each brother carried a half until they caught a taxi to the museum. On their way into Cairo, they had to pay a fee to customs officers, who classed the mummy as 'pickled fish'.

The battle against the tomb robbers was far from won, however. In 1898, archaeologist Victor Loret discovered a second secret store in the Valley of the Kings. Even though the cache had been looted in ancient times, the mummy of the pharaoh had been left alone. At last, the body of an Egyptian king had been found exactly as it was meant to be. Nine other mummies were found in a side-chamber, and on the floors of the two rooms were a mass of objects: statues, vases and

wooden models of animals and birds. It was an incredible discovery, but word spread quickly and a gang of robbers – perhaps the very guards hired by Loret to protect the tomb – tore the pharaoh's body to pieces as they hunted for jewels.

Emptying the Royal Cache

Horse Sense

We can thank our four-legged friends for some major discoveries:

- **The Tomb of the Door of the Horse**
  In 1899, Howard Carter's horse stumbled and exposed a shaft in the ground. Looking closer, Carter found a sealed chamber. The coffin inside had no name but next to it he found a statue of the 2nd-Dynasty king Mentuhotep.

- **The Tombs of the Pyramid Builders**
  In August 1990, an American woman was riding a horse near the Sphinx in Giza when her horse tripped over a pile of mud bricks and threw her. The mud-brick wall turned out to be a tomb, with a long **vaulted** chamber and two false doors. Archaeologists later found 600 graves and 30 larger tombs. The horse had stumbled on one of the largest ancient Egyptian cemeteries ever found!

- **The Valley of the Golden Mummies**
  In 1996, an antiquities guard was riding his donkey across the desert at Bahariya Oasis when it hit its leg on the edge of a tomb. Four tombs were excavated and 105 mummies from the Roman period were found inside. Many were covered in gold and very well preserved despite being over 2,000 years old. So far, some 10,000 mummies have been found in other tombs nearby.

Early archaeologists were surprisingly brutal. Auguste Mariette used explosives to blast open tombs and Émile Amelineau boasted that he smashed any jars he couldn't sell. However, a more careful approach was taken by British archaeologist Sir Flinders Petrie, known as the 'Father of Modern Egyptology'. Petrie prided himself on paying attention to the smallest detail, whether it was a piece of broken pottery or a strand of hair. He used large gangs of workers, carefully lifting heavy blocks away using pulleys.

Arriving in Egypt in 1880, Petrie spent the next 46 years trying to undo the damage done by previous Egyptologists,[5] as well as making some spectacular finds, including the tombs of the first pharaohs and the mummy of High Priest Ranefer (at the time, the oldest ever found). He claimed everything he found and shipped an enormous number of mummies and other historical objects to museums in Britain, Europe and the United States.

5. *When he died in 1942, Petrie, always the scientist, donated his head to the Royal College of Surgeons. Due to the Second World War, it was kept in a jar for a few years until it could be moved safely!*

Tutmania!

In the early 20th century, archaeologists still hoped to find a royal tomb in the Valley of the Kings with its treasures still in place. Then, in 1922, British archaeologist Howard Carter made a spectacular find – the tomb of King Tutankhamun. He uncovered a flight of steps leading to an unexplored burial chamber. Breaking through the sealed door, he found the body of the ancient pharaoh lying in a solid gold coffin. The tomb had already been broken into twice, but it was still packed with the king's treasure.

Carter was meticulous in his studies. It took many weeks, but every object was photographed, mapped, described and sketched before being carefully wrapped and put in storage. The discovery was a sensation and made headlines all over the world. Carter was inundated by telegrams and letters, and hundreds of tourists waited outside the tomb for a peek. Hundreds more tried to get a tour of the tomb, getting in Carter's way and slowing down the work.

The Natural Scream

When he saw the twisted face of a mummy from the Royal Cache in the late 19th century, anatomist Daniel Fouquet wrote: 'The last convulsions of horrid agony can, after thousands of years, still be seen.' There's no doubt that some mummies appear to be screaming or grimacing in agony, leading to wild stories about horrific deaths.

Edvard Munch's famous painting 'The Scream' is said to have been inspired by a Peruvian mummy. The truth is, the mummy's 'scream' is just the jaw dropping down naturally after death as the muscles relax and start to rot. In ancient China, some mummies were given chinstraps to stop their jaws from gaping open – modern morticians use a needle and thread!

In the afterlife, no-one can hear you scream!

The discovery of Tutankhamun's tomb led to a new craze, 'Tutmania', which influenced a new style of decoration known as **Art Deco**. Soon, Egyptian-style clothes were incredibly fashionable. Even architecture was affected as Egyptian designs were copied in buildings such as cinemas.

In the last 50 years there have been many other important discoveries, such as the Animal Cemetery and New Kingdom tombs found at Saqqara and the tomb of the sons of Ramesses II. Today, Egyptian and international teams often work together, but problems with looting remain. When Egyptian archaeologist Zahi Hawass discovered the Valley of the Golden Mummies in 1996, he kept it a secret for three years to stop the tombs from being plundered.

The Mummy's Curse

The excitement over the discovery of Tutankhamun's tomb intensified when Lord Carnarvon, who had funded the expedition, suddenly became ill from an infected mosquito bite on his cheek. Within a week he was dead and newspapers were soon filled with stories about a 'curse'. Yet Howard Carter, who spent more time than anyone else inside Tut's tomb, lived another 17 years!

Poor King Tutankhamun had every right to be turning in his grave. By the time Howard Carter had unwrapped him, his body was in pieces. Carter also put Tut's mummy back in his coffin without even tucking him in. The true extent of the damage was only revealed in 1968 when the naked monarch was removed again for X-ray.

The tomb is discovered

King Tut's Revenge?

Newspapers tried to link anything and everything to the opening of the tomb:

• A writer, Marie Corelli, blamed Carnarvon's death on ancient poisons in the tomb.

• 'Death shall come on swift wings to him who disturbs the peace of the king' was one of four spells inscribed on 'magic bricks' inside Tut's tomb. It comes from chapter 151 of *The Book of the Dead*.

• At the exact moment Carnarvon died, his dog Susie howled and died back in England (though this would have been in the middle of the night, English time).

• Howard Carter's pet canary is said to have been eaten by a cobra just as Carter discovered the steps to the tomb.

• Prince Ali Fahmy Bey, a visitor to the tomb, was later shot by his wife, but Tut's curse was blamed for his death.

• Collectors wondered where the curse was going to strike next. Some buried unwanted bits of mummy in their garden or threw them into rivers. Others posted them to the British Museum, which was swamped with parcels.

Mummy's curse or natural selection? Carter's canary comes to a sssssticky end!

The mummy's curse was a popular story long before Tutankhamun's grave was found. A book by the scholar Jean Bodin, completed around 1588, said that mummies smuggled out of Egypt were believed to cause storms at sea, so crews were flinging them overboard to avoid being shipwrecked.

In fact, few curses have been found written on the walls of tombs, and the only real danger comes from infectious micro-organisms. In 1973, 12 archaeologists opened the tomb of King Casimir IV of Poland, who died in 1492. Within a few days, just two of the researchers were still alive. When one of the survivors bravely examined the tomb again, he found poisonous fungi that were probably responsible for the deaths of his 10 colleagues.

In 1999, Gotthard Kramer, a German microbiologist, studied 40 mummies and found several dangerous mould **spores**. He argued that when tombs are first opened, the fresh air could disturb these spores, causing a hazard for anyone working inside the tomb.

162

Unlucky Mummy

A mummy of a priestess who died in 950 BC was bought by four British tourists when they visited Egypt in the 1860s. All four of them died soon afterwards. The mummy was then given to the British Museum, and the man who delivered it died within a week. A photographer who took a picture of the mummy was supposedly so spooked by the image that he killed himself. By 1909, the mummy had such a scary reputation that it had to be locked away. But the wild stories continued – one rumour suggested this 'unlucky' mummy was sold to an American and was on the *Titanic* when it went down in 1912.

'Right, how are we going to explain this one?'

'Err... mummy's curse?'

Five Real Curses

Some of these curses may have been aimed at *Ka* priests to make sure they protected the tomb and fed the mummy's *ka* properly, rather than as a warning to robbers.

**'Anyone who enters this tomb:
I shall wring his neck like a bird.'**
from the tomb of Hermeru,
High Priest to King Unis (5th Dynasty)

'He shall be eaten by a crocodile and snake.'
from the tomb of royal dentists Iy Mry,
Kem Msw and Sekhem Ka (5th Dynasty)

**'He shall be cooked together
with the condemned.'**
from the tomb of King Meryibre Khety
(First Intermediate Period)

'He shall have no heir.'
from the tomb of King Tuthmosis I
(18th Dynasty)

'He shall be miserable and persecuted.'
from the tomb of Penniut, high priest of the
Pharaoh Ramesses II (19th Dynasty)

CHAPTER FIVE

UNWRAPPING THE SECRETS

CSI: Egypt

One of the things that makes Egyptian mummies so fascinating is the fact that they're wrapped up like a parcel – and we'd all love to know what lies beneath the bandages. The first unwrappings were mostly done for fun in front of large audiences. Unfortunately, the unwrappers often hacked through the linen wrappings, destroying a great deal of scientific evidence.

165

Even when the intentions were good, the methods were often clumsy. When French Egyptologist Jean-François Champollion and his brother had finished examining a mummy in the 1820s, they rewrapped it with its arms crossed. This caused such a strain on the crumbling body that the chest and arms were badly damaged and the fragile feet fell off. When the Royal Cache of mummies was discovered in 1881, the Egyptologists were so eager to see the faces of the royal pharaohs and queens that they didn't take any notes about the mummies' wrappings.

From the 1900s, Egyptologists began to use modern scientific methods. A mummy would be treated in the same way as a murder victim. Forensic scientists looked for the cause of death and whether the mummy was diseased or ill while alive. In 1907, the British Egyptologist Margaret Murray did the first scientific study of two mummies from the Middle Kingdom. She had a team of doctors, chemists and cloth specialists all working together. By the 1930s, scientists were able to work out a mummy's blood group, and chemical tests revealed what had been used to preserve the mummy. Egyptologists finally had something to compare with ancient accounts of how the mummymakers worked.

When German scientist Wilhelm Konrad Roentgen discovered X-rays in 1895, at last there was a way to explore mummies without butchering them. In 1903, Tuthmosis IV became the first royal mummy to be X-rayed.[1] The first X-rays were weak and only the feet and hands could be examined. By the 1920s and 30s, they were often used to locate precious amulets and jewellery, but from the 1950s archaeologists were more interested in finding out how the mummies had died.

By the time Tutankhamun was X-rayed in 1968, scanning machines were far more advanced.

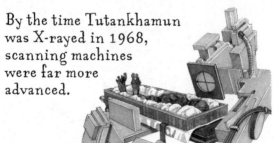

1. Sir Grafton Elliot Smith used a horse-drawn carriage to carry Tuthmosis' mummy from the Cairo Museum to the private nursing home where the X-ray machine was.

167

In recent years, studies on human genes have also given us a better idea of what the ancient Egyptians looked like – not that different from Egyptians today, it turns out. In 2005, scientists even created a bust of King Tutankhamun based on 3-D **CT** scans of his 3,300-year-old mummy. The result looked remarkably similar to a famous painting of the pharaoh as a child.

Ten Ways to Study a Mummy

Have you ever wished that you could unwrap a mummy? The scientists who investigate mummies today are like detectives looking for historical clues, but there are now ways to do this without needing to unwrap or damage them in any way. Many tests can be done in the mummy's resting place, so that mummies do not have to be removed from their tomb.

While CT scans and endoscopy leave the mummy undamaged, **DNA** tests require a small sample of tissue to be taken from the mummy.[2] Other samples from around the body, such as linen, dust particles and plaster, can be carbon-dated, giving an accurate date for the mummy.

1. Clean the Body

Every mummy needs a good clean before it is examined, especially mummies with a crusty layer of sand. This can be a delicate operation as ancient bodies are so crumbly!

---

2. *Some museums ban this. A DNA test was carried out on Ramesses II only because a loose hair was found at the bottom of his coffin when it arrived in Paris in 1975.*

Before you go too far, it's worth making a few basic checks to ensure that the mummy in front of you isn't a fake. During the 19th century there were many fake mummies created by dealers to part gullible tourists from their money. Many mummies of 'children' turn out to be animals such as baboons, or a bundle of packing materials.

2. Observation – Look and Learn

A well-trained eye can learn a lot just by looking at a mummy:

- How and when was it preserved? Look at the general state of the mummy and its colour.

- How did he or she die? Broken bones or a smashed skull could indicate a violent death in battle.

- Were they rich? Very soft feet may show that the mummy was carried everywhere while alive – perhaps its servants did all the running around.

- Was he a priest? While most Egyptians shaved their scalps and wore wigs, a priest had to shave off all his body hair – even the eyebrows.

170

- How long did he or she live? Young children still have their 'milk' teeth, young adult teeth are more ground down thanks to the gritty Egyptian bread, while adults in their early 20s often have wisdom teeth poking through their gums.

- Any signs of rotting? Have a sniff and look for holes made by beetles and other insects burrowing into the coffin or the mummy!

- Anything else unusual? The skin on one 11th-Dynasty mummy is so well preserved you can see tattoos. Mummies from the 12th-Dynasty often have beards – a fashion that didn't last.

Taking photographs allows you to keep a record of how the mummy looks. It's easy to get distracted if a mummy has a particularly beautiful or gruesome face, so remember to get good pictures of the whole body and record anything unusual. If the shape of the coffin makes it hard to take a picture, an accurate drawing is an excellent back-up.

3. Endoscopy – An Inside Look

An endoscope is another great way to explore a mummy, but what is it? Think 'bend-o-scope' – it's a long bendy tube tipped with a mini video camera that allows you to explore right inside the body. The tube contains tiny glass fibres (as thin as hairs) that carry digital information as pulses of light. The camera can be used to find what organs were left inside the body by embalmers and can even collect bits of tissue for other tests. However, you may need to make a small cut in the mummy's chest to fit the endoscope in.

4. Scanning

X-rays can show a lot more than broken bones. They reveal whether mummies are male or female, and uncover mummymaking tricks, such as using sticks to join a wonky head back to the body. A mis-shapen skull can be a sign of diseases such as arthritis and smallpox, while the growth lines in bones give a good idea of how healthy the mummy was in life. X-rays made on paper rather than film, known as xeroradiographs, are better at picking out the edges of objects, so they're

good for spotting amulets and jewellery under bandages. CT scans combine powerful X-ray equipment with computers. They take thousands of cross-sections of the inside of the body. When the pictures are put together they create a 3D picture of a body or face. While X-rays show only the bones, CT scans also reveal the mummy's skin, soft flesh and linen bandages. They're also powerful enough to scan inside a mummy while it's still in its case.

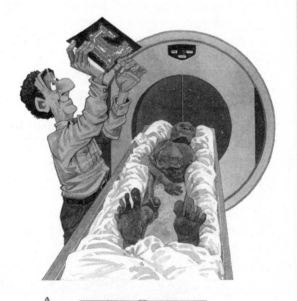

5. Hair samples

Looking closely at hairs with microscopes or testing them with chemicals can also reveal amazing details about mummies. For instance, the hair colour of mummies or buried bodies can change. Ramesses II, for example, had white hair when he died at 90, but tests showed he had red hair as a young man, as traces of hair colour remain in the roots even in old age. Hair samples taken from mummies of children in the Andes mountains have shown that children as young as 6 years old were 'fattened up' before being sacrificed. They were drugged then left to freeze to death.

6. Rehydrating

A sample tissue from a mummy can be rehydrated (made wet again) and studied under a microscope. By looking at a slice of its liver, a scientist can spot if a mummy had diseases such as schistosomiasis, caused by worms living in the waters of the Nile. Studying the disease in the past may help doctors treat it today.

Diseased, Bitten and Just Worn Out

Studies on mummies reveal that life wasn't always rosy in ancient Egypt:

- **Arthritis** – Ramesses II, Amenophis II and several other pharaohs suffered from this disease that causes pain in the joints.
- **Malaria** – This deadly disease spread by mosquito bites has also been found in tissue samples.
- **Lungs** – These were damaged from breathing in the smoke from fires and oil lamps.
- **Typhoid** – A seven-year-old girl found in the Dush necropolis wore a wig after typhoid, an illness caused by bacteria in infected food or water, caused her hair to fall out.
- **Smallpox** – Several bumps on Ramesses V's face and a nasty rash on his body show that he probably died from smallpox.
- **Fractures/Injuries** – Sixty soldiers buried near Mentuhotep II were killed in battle by arrows in the eye, having their skulls crushed, or being chopped in the face by an axe.
- **A Tough Life** – Studies on almost 700 mummies from the Dush necropolis show that most had very hard lives and poor health.
- **Worn Gnashers** – Most Egyptians had appalling teeth, as sand from the desert got into their bread and ground their teeth down.

7. Fingerprinting

Over the years, different techniques have been used to get fingerprints from the dead. One approach is to cut off the fingers then soak or inject them with various solutions to make the fingerprints clearer. Other scientists have coated the tips of the fingers with dental paste to make casts. These are then painted and printed.

8. Blood

Blood tests showed that an unknown mummy found in the Valley of the Kings could be related to Tutankhamun. But such tests can be unclear, as samples are often contaminated by the herbs and spices used by the embalmers to preserve the body. British and American scientists are now working together to create the world's first Mummy Bank in Manchester, England, which will store samples of blood, tissue and internal organs from mummies around the world.

9. DNA

DNA carries a person's genetic code, so matching two sets of DNA can show if two mummies are related. Human DNA survives long after death and it can be taken from teeth, bone or hair. It has even been recovered from a fossil 70,000 years old. However, scientists must take great care as it is easy to contaminate samples with their own DNA. A DNA testing unit has been set up at the Cairo Museum to compare the DNA of royal mummies. It has already proved that King Tutankhamun's wife was his sister and that the two baby mummies found in his tomb were his.

10. Dating

There are two main ways of finding out how old an ancient object is. The first is to compare it with an object from the same period; this is known as 'relative dating'. Egyptian sculptures are particularly useful for this as the names of their owners were usually carved on them.

The second method is carbon dating, but how does it work? While you are alive, your body takes in carbon from the air. But when you die, one form of carbon, Carbon 14, begins to decay, while another, Carbon 12, remains the same. By comparing how much Carbon 14 there is to Carbon 12, scientists can work out how long something has been dead. Unfortunately, carbon dating is only useful on mummies buried after 500 BC as with older mummies the results are not accurate enough.

The Tourist Trap

In 1934 newspapers told how a Hungarian tourist got lost in the tomb of Ramesses II in the Valley of the Kings. After spending a night in the pitch-dark tomb she was so spooked that she couldn't speak when she was found the next morning under a statue of the pharaoh.

The Mystery Continues

Despite the wonders of modern science, mummies remain as mysterious as ever. Egyptian mummies have been unwrapped, sliced up, prodded and X-rayed, but the ritual remains a secret, known only to the priests who carried out the process all those centuries ago.

We need to remind ourselves just how amazing it is that mummies survive. These bundles of linen, dried flesh and bone are five or six thousand years old. There simply isn't much that survives that long. The films, papers and photos we use use to remember people today probably wouldn't survive either.

So when you look at a mummy, forget that it looks like a wrinkly old prune. You're staring into the face of someone who was alive thousands of years ago. Now that really is very peculiar…

Where Are They Now (and What's Left)?

- **Djer** – Only the mummified wrist of Djer was found. Not realising it was an important find, the head of the Cairo museum, Émile Brugsch, threw away the wrist along with the bandages.

- **Tuthmosis III** – After being ripped apart by grave robbers, Tuthmosis III's mummy was so badly damaged that the priests who repaired it had to use wooden splints to hold it together. He currently rests in the Cairo Museum.

- **Tutankhamun** – Although it was in very good condition when it was discovered, Tutankhamun's mummy was badly mauled by Howard Carter when he unwrapped it. Tut is now back in his tomb in the Valley of the Kings.

- **Queen Ahmose-Nefertari** – When she died during the reign of Tuthmosis I the Queen was buried in the royal necropolis in Thebes. Later the mummy was buried in the Royal Cache at Deir el-Bahri, where it was found in 1881. Her body supposedly ponged so much that Émile Brugsch had it reburied in the museum gardens in Cairo. However, it was later dug up and examined. She now rests in the Cairo Museum.

- **Ramesses I** – The body of Ramesses I was probably snatched from the Royal Cache at Deir-El-Bahri. In 1860 it was sold for £7 to a Canadian doctor called James Douglas, who bought the mummy for a museum in Niagara Falls. For 140 years, the mummy was displayed as part of a freak show including a two-headed calf and a five-legged pig! In 1999, the mummy was sold to another museum, in Atlanta, USA, where a CT scan revealed a strong family resemblance to Seti I and Ramesses II. He now resides back in Egypt.

- **Seti I** – Though one of the best-preserved mummies, Seti I had his head ripped from his body and his back caved in by tomb robbers. His current home is the Cairo Museum.

- **Ramesses II** – In 1974, Ramesses II became the only royal mummy to have travelled with its own passport! His occupation was listed as 'King (Deceased)'. French Egyptologists visiting his tomb noticed he was beginning to rot, so they transported him to France for treatment. When he arrived at Le Bourget airport, just outside Paris, he was greeted with full military honours! In Paris he was successfully treated for fungal infection. He is now back in Cairo.

TIMELINE

c. 5000 BC People settle along the Nile Delta.

c. 3200 BC Hieroglyphics developed.

c. 3100 BC Narmer joins Upper and Lower Egypt.

2890–2686 BC Wooden coffins used and corpses wrapped in resin.

2686 BC Step Pyramid at Saqqara built by Djoser.

2550–2490 BC Khufu, Khafre and Menkaure build great pyramids.

2160 BC Capital of Egypt moves from Memphis to Herakleopolis.

2135–1986 BC Egypt split into north and south, ruled from Herakleopolis and Thebes respectively.

2134–2000 BC Capital moved to Thebes. Egypt reunited by Mentuhotep II.

1956 BC Senusret I begins to build temple of Karnak at Thebes.

1937–1756 BC Amenemhet moves capital back to Memphis.

1700 BC Earliest evidence of diagnostic medicine in Egypt.

1650 BC Capital yet again moved to Thebes.

1333–1324 BC Reign of Tutankhamun.

1186–1089 BC Royal tombs in the Valley of the Kings plundered for treasure by robbers.

1069–1043 BC Noticeable improvement of mummification techniques.

525–404 BC Persians invade and rule Egypt until forced out by Amyrtaeus in 404 BC.

332 BC Alexander the great invades Egypt and founds Alexandria.

300 BC Temple of Isis built on island of Philae in the Nile River.

31 BC Queen Cleopatra and her lover, Roman general Mark Antony, are defeated by Octavian, who begins Roman rule of Egypt.

AD 395 Egyptian Hieroglyphics no longer used or understood.

c.AD 1000 Practice of 'eating mummy' begins.

1799 Napoleonic forces discover the Rosetta Stone.

1822 Jean-François Champollion decodes hieroglyphics using the Rosetta Stone.

1834 First public mummy unwrapping performed by Dr. Thomas J. Pettigrew.

1836 Auguste Mariette sets up Cairo Museum.

1842 Prussian explorer Richard Lepsius leads an Egyptian expedition, making detailed studies of the pyramids of Giza and the Valley of the Kings.

1880 Flinders Petrie arrives in Egypt to begin the serious study of Egyptology.

1881 Discovery of Royal Cache at Deir el-Bahri.

1907 Margaret Murray performs the first scientific study of mummies from the Middle Kingdom.

1922 Archaeologist Howard Carter discovers the tomb of King Tutankhamun.

1996 Zahi Hawass discovers the Valley of the Golden Mummies.

2005 Scientists create a bust of King Tutankhamun based on 3-D CT scans of his 3,300-year-old mummy.

GLOSSARY

antiquities – artifacts from the ancient world.

Art Deco – an international art design movement involving symmetry and parallel lines.

bier – a stand on which a corpse, coffin or casket is placed to be carried to the grave.

bitumen – also known as asphalt or tar, bitumen is a black, oily material that occurs naturally as a by-product of decomposed organic materials.

cholera – a disease transmitted by bacteria-filled water.

coppersmith – a person who makes objects from copper.

Coptic – a later form of the Egyptian language. It is estimated that around 300 people speak it today.

CT – also known as a CAT scan, a CT (computed tomography) scan uses special X-ray equipment and sophisticated computers to diagnose and treat medical conditions.

delta – a triangle of organic material deposited at the mouth of a river where it enters a large body of water, such as an ocean.

DNA (deoxyribonucleic acid) – a material which holds genetic information about a living creature.

dyke – a long wall built to keep out the sea.

dynasty – period of time in ancient Egyptian history in which Egypt was ruled by kings and queens from the same family.

Egyptologist – a person who studies the archaeology and ancient history of Egypt.

epitaph – a short text honouring a deceased person,

festering – rotting.

foreman – the person in charge of a construction site.

henna – a plant which can be used to stain skin or hair temporarily, as a form of body art or tattooing.

heretic – someone who introduces a change in an established religion.

ibis – a long-legged wading bird.

mason – a worker who builds with brick or stone.

papyrus – the reed that Egyptians used to make paper for scrolls (plural **papyri**)

sarcophagus – a container for a corpse, usually carved from rock or stone.

scourge – a cause of great trouble and affliction.

spores – tiny cellular structures that fungi use to reproduce.

vaulted – arched.

INDEX

A

accidental mummy 11, 45, 46, 50, 51
Aha 100, 104
Akh 35–43, 75
Akhenaten 22, 116
Alexander the Great 8, 84, 184
Alexandria 13, 84, 145, 184
Amenemhet 27, 33, 127, 183
Amenhotep I 22, 89
Amenhotep III 70
Amun Re 25, 81, 89, 108, 114, 136
animal mummies 88–94
antiquities 149, 154, 186
Anubis 32, 42, 62, 77, 93
Apis bull 90
Arabic 9, 87, 116
Art Deco 158, 186
Aswan 120, 144, 148

B

Ba 35, 36, 43, 80
bacteria 11, 47, 53, 67, 175
Belzoni, Giovanni Battista 142, 143

Bentham, Jeremy 8
bier 95, 97, 186
bitumen 9, 10, 60, 93, 137, 140, 186
Book of the Dead, The 39–41, 86, 103, 112, 145, 160
brain 56, 64, 65
bribery 131, 134, 135
Brugsch, Émile 149, 152, 180
Bubastis 91, 94

C

Cairo 115, 120, 127, 145, 149, 152, 167, 177, 180, 181, 184
canopic jars 68, 83, 97, 130
Carnarvon, Lord 159, 160
Carter, Howard 67, 154, 156, 159, 160, 180, 185
Champollion, Jean-François 146, 166, 184
cholera 150, 186
Christianity 58, 137
Cleopatra VII 13, 21, 22, 184
Coffin Texts 39
Coming Forth by Day 39
Coptic 10, 186

curse 62, 159–164
CT 168, 169, 173, 181, 185, 186

D

Deir el-Bahri 136, 149, 180, 181, 185
Deir el-Medina 116, 117, 126, 132, 133
disease 140, 141, 166, 172, 174, 175
Djer 54, 104, 180
Djoser 105, 106, 182
DNA 169, 177

E

Egyptology 14, 46, 54, 67, 126, 144, 155, 166, 167, 181, 185, 187
embalming 15, 32, 43, 45, 52, 45–78, 81, 131
endoscopy 169, 172
explorers 142–147, 156, 184, 185

F

failed mummies 70, 71
fake mummies 91, 140, 141, 148, 170
false eyes 67, 86
farming 18, 23, 37
fashion 27, 147, 158
Fields of Reeds 35–38, 41, 43
films 14, 78

food 20, 25, 26, 29, 34, 36, 47, 98, 100, 101, 119, 151, 175,
forensic science 166, 169–178

G

Giza 22, 26, 142, 143, 145, 154, 185,
grave goods 33, 48, 97, 99–104, 130, 149

H

Hagens, Gunther von 53
hair 8, 27, 46, 47, 56, 70, 75, 77, 144, 155, 169, 170, 174, 175, 177
Hapy 24, 68
Hathor 39, 41
Hawass, Zahi 126, 158, 185

heart 29, 4, 42, 46, 65, 72, 77, 151
henna 75, 187
Henttawi 70, 131
Herodotus 13, 21, 60, 90, 115, 137
hieroglyphics 13, 26, 146, 182, 184
Horus 42, 68, 74, 87
human sacrifice 104, 174

I

ibis 89, 91, 187
Imhotep 91, 105, 106, 116
incense 66, 98, 109
inscription 33, 34, 103, 146, 160
Intermediate Periods 21, 87
invasion 18, 21, 58, 142, 183, 184
Isis 32, 41, 87, 184

K

Ka 35, 36, 43, 45, 54, 80, 98, 99, 101, 125, 164
Karnak 25, 183
Khafre 22, 111, 182
Khufu 22, 111, 182

L

Lepsius, Richard 145, 185
linen 12, 55, 62, 68, 72, 75, 76, 78, 80, 86, 109, 134, 14 0, 165, 169, 173, 179
Luxor 112

M

Macbeth 138
magic 15, 24, 25, 32, 34, 37, 39, 41, 62, 67, 74, 76–81, 84, 86, 98–102, 160
make-up 20, 27, 67, 75, 100

mask 8, 12, 33, 52, 62, 80, 129
Mariette, Auguste 149, 155, 184
mastaba 106, 108
medicine 137–140, 183
Mediterranean 18, 148
Meidum 108
Memphis 90, 182, 183
Menkaure 111, 148
Mentuhotep I 154
Mentuhotep II 175, 183
Middle Kingdom 21, 30, 36, 39, 57, 84, 102, 104, 108, 126, 166, 185
mortuary temple 102, 109
mourners 97
mumiya 9, 10, 60
Murray, Margaret 166, 185
museums
  British Museum 8, 146, 160, 163
  Cairo Museum 149, 152, 167, 177, 180, 181, 184
  Egyptian Museum, Berlin 22, 116, 145
  Leiden Museum 91
  Louvre, The 145

N

Napoleon 142, 144, 145, 184
Narmer 20, 21, 23, 105, 182
natron 50, 61, 66, 68, 72, 74
necropolis 37, 93, 112, 122, 130, 175, 180
Nefertiti 22, 116
New Kingdom 21, 23, 32, 38, 39, 57, 86, 87, 112, 114, 126, 158
Nile 13, 17–20, 23, 32, 61, 90, 95, 112, 120, 132, 134, 144, 174, 182, 184

O

obsidian 62
Old Kingdom 21, 30, 37, 39, 57, 84, 102, 124, 152,
organs 33, 46, 47, 55, 60, 62, 65, 68, 77, 172, 176, 186
Osiris 30, 32, 35, 36, 39, 42, 61, 65, 81, 82, 128
Otherworld 29–39, 42, 44, 57, 77, 95, 100, 102, 103, 111, 112, 128
Ötzi the Iceman 50

P

papyrus 41, 80, 86, 133, 135, 187

Papyrus of Ani, The 41
Petrie, Flinders 54, 56, 155, 185
Pettigrew, Thomas J. 147
pit graves 48, 54, 105, 124
plastination 53
plumb-line 27
prayer 25, 35, 61, 81, 109
Ptah 41, 90
pyramid 21, 22, 26, 30, 91, 105, 106, 108, 109, 111, 112, 115, 116, 124, 125, 127, 133, 142, 143, 145, 154, 182, 185
Pyramid Texts 39, 55, 94, 111, 152

R

Ramesses I 114, 142, 181
Ramesses II 22, 75, 90, 102, 113, 120, 129, 135, 158, 164, 174, 175, 178, 181
Ramesses III 14, 102, 6
Ramesses V 175
Ramesses IX 132, 133, 136,
Ranefer 56, 155
resin 53, 55, 58, 60, 64, 67–72, 76, 78, 89, 93, 138, 182
rituals 87

robbery 15, 54, 56, 81,
84, 88, 111, 112, 114,
120, 121, 122,
124–136, 142, 152,
153, 164, 181, 183,
Romans 13, 21, 22,
58, 154, 184
Rosetta Stone 146,
184
Royal Cache 136, 149,
152, 153, 157, 166,
180, 181, 185

S
Sahara 17, 38
Saqqara 26, 91, 106,
138, 141, 152, 158,
182
sarcophagus 12, 84,
86, 90, 114, 122, 127,
134, 143, 148
scarab 65, 77, 82, 102,
149
Senusret I 125, 183
servants 35, 97, 102,
104, 106, 116, 117,
135, 170
Seth 32, 74, 128
Seti I 57, 104, 113,
142, 181
shabtis 102–104, 114
Siculus, Diodorus 13,
137
Sobek 90, 91
sphinx 22, 154
stalls 78
star map 26, 27
Step pyramid 26, 106,
108, 116, 182

T
Thebes 70, 112, 132,
134, 180, 182, 183
traps 15, 111, 125–127,
treasure 8, 15, 81, 114,
120, 121, 124, 128,
129, 134, 137, 143,
149, 156, 183
Tutankhamun 8, 9, 12,
17, 67, 80, 81, 84, 89,
100, 102, 104, 120,
129, 130, 156, 158,
159, 162, 168, 176,
177, 180, 183, 185

V
Valley of the Kings
112, 114, 116, 117,
119, 126, 136, 142,
145, 152, 154, 156,
158, 176, 178, 180,
183, 185
Victorians 13, 14, 147,
vizier 26, 117, 118,
135

X
X-rays 14, 71, 93, 94,
159, 167, 172, 173,
179, 186